International Boundaries in a Global Era

As we move deeper into the twenty-first century, the forces of globalisation continue to transform both the spaces around international borders, and the social processes, cultural practices, economies, and political dynamics within and between these spaces. The geographies of border regions have undergone a dramatic transformation over the last half century; nation-state boundaries are growing ever more porous in many (though not all) areas of the planet. Global trade has become an accepted norm in business transactions almost everywhere. Coupled with the revolution in digital technology, the era of globalisation promises to continue to challenge old ideas, with new approaches to understanding international boundaries and the regions they impact.

All of the chapters in this book, mainly drawn from the US–Mexico border (with comparisons to Europe), speak to the ways in which border regions have become important places in their own right, spaces where people live, work, and create art, where corporations invest, where crimes occur, and where security remains a concern. They are, therefore, spaces that need to be better understood and managed, especially in light of the cross-national and global forces impinging upon them.

This book was originally published as a special issue of *Global Society*.

Lawrence A. Herzog is a Professor in the Graduate Program in City Planning, School of Public Affairs, San Diego State University, California, USA. He is also a consultant and writer specialising in planning, sustainable development, and urban design in the United States, Mexico, and Latin America. He has written or edited ten books on urban planning, design, and global/cross-border development.

Keith J. Hayward is Professor of Criminology, and Deputy Director of Learning and Teaching in the School of Social Policy, Sociology and Social Research at the University of Kent, Canterbury, UK. He is author, co-author, and editor of ten books, including *Cultural Criminology: An Invitation* (2015).

International Boundaries in a Global Era

Cross-border space, place and society in the twenty-first century

Edited by

Lawrence A. Herzog and Keith J. Hayward

LONDON AND NEW YORK

First published 2016
by Routledge
2 Park Square, Milton Park, Abingdon, Oxon, OX14 4RN, UK

and by Routledge
711 Third Avenue, New York, NY 10017, USA

First issued in paperback 2017

Routledge is an imprint of the Taylor & Francis Group, an informa business

British Library Cataloguing in Publication Data
A catalogue record for this book is available from the British Library

ISBN 13: 978-1-138-29520-9 (pbk)
ISBN 13: 978-1-138-95054-2 (hbk)

Typeset in Palatino
by RefineCatch Limited, Bungay, Suffolk

Publisher's Note
The publisher accepts responsibility for any inconsistencies that may have arisen during the conversion of this book from journal articles to book chapters, namely the possible inclusion of journal terminology.

Disclaimer
Every effort has been made to contact copyright holders for their permission to reprint material in this book. The publishers would be grateful to hear from any copyright holder who is not here acknowledged and will undertake to rectify any errors or omissions in future editions of this book.

Contents

Citation Information

The chapters in this book were originally published in *Global Society*, volume 28, issue 4 (October 2014). When citing this material, please use the original page numbering for each article, as follows:

Chapter 1
Globalisation, Place and Twenty-First-Century International Border Regions: An Introduction to the Special Issue
Lawrence A. Herzog
Global Society, volume 28, issue 4 (October 2014) pp. 391–397

Chapter 2
Trade and Environmental Protection along the United States–Mexico Border
Stephen P. Mumme
Global Society, volume 28, issue 4 (October 2014) pp. 398–418

Chapter 3
One Bioregion/One Health: An Integrative Narrative for Transboundary Planning along the US–Mexico Border
Keith Pezzoli, Justine Kozo, Karen Ferran, Wilma Wooten, Gudelia Rangel Gomez and Wael K. Al-Delaimy
Global Society, volume 28, issue 4 (October 2014) pp. 419–440

Chapter 4
The Cross-Border Metropolis in a Global Age: A Conceptual Model and Empirical Evidence from the US–Mexico and European Border Regions
Lawrence A. Herzog and Christophe Sohn
Global Society, volume 28, issue 4 (October 2014) pp. 441–461

Chapter 5
Policing the Workplace and Rebuilding the State in "America's Finest City": US Immigration Control in the San Diego, California–Mexico Borderlands
Joseph Nevins
Global Society, volume 28, issue 4 (October 2014) pp. 462–482

Chapter 6

Solving the Border Paradox? Border Security, Economic Integration and the Mérida Initiative
Paul Ashby
Global Society, volume 28, issue 4 (October 2014) pp. 483–508

For any permission-related enquiries please visit:
http://www.tandfonline.com/page/help/permissions

Notes on Contributors

Wael K. Al-Delaimy is Professor and Chief of the Division of Global Health in the Department of Family and Preventive Medicine, University of California – San Diego, CA, USA. His work is focused on environmental epidemiology and exposure assessment, and in the US–Mexico border area he has worked on pesticide exposure among farm workers. Prior to his current appointment, he was a scientist at the International Agency for Research on Cancer in Lyon, France, and Post-Doctoral Research Associate at the Harvard School of Public Health, Cambridge, MA, USA.

Paul Ashby is a PhD candidate and Associate Lecturer at the University of Kent, Canterbury, UK. His thesis research focuses on contemporary US foreign policy towards Mexico, especially regarding the Mérida Initiative and Mexico's drug violence. He lectures on Ethics in International Relations.

Karen Ferran is the former Chief Epidemiologist/Program Manager of the Early Warning Infectious Disease Surveillance Program of the California Department of Public Health. Her work focuses on pandemic influenza, emerging and re-emerging pathogens, and agents of bioterrorism. She co-founded One Border One Health, and is co-chair of the Surveillance Committee. She is a Lecturer at San Diego State University, California, USA, in the Graduate School of Public Health, and is currently developing the One Health curriculum.

Lawrence A. Herzog is Professor in the Graduate Program in City Planning, School of Public Affairs, San Diego State University, San Diego, California, USA. He is also a consultant and writer specialising in planning and urban design in the United States, Mexico, and Latin America. He has written or edited 10 books on planning, environmental design, and global/cross-border development. His latest book is *Global Suburbs: Urban Sprawl from the Rio Grande to Rio de Janeiro* (Routledge, 2014).

Justine Kozo is Chief of the Office of Border Health for the County of San Diego, Health and Human Services Agency, California, USA. Under her direction, the office aims to increase communication and collaboration among organisations working in the California–Baja California border region to address public health concerns. In collaboration with the California Office of Binational Border Health, she also facilitates meetings and activities of the Border Health Consortium of the Californias.

Stephen P. Mumme is Professor of Political Science at Colorado State University, Fort Collins, Colorado, USA, where his research centres on trans-boundary environmental management in North America. He is the author or co-author of various monographs, including *Statecraft, Domestic Politics, and Foreign Policy: The El Chamizal Dispute* (1988), as well as numerous chapters and journal articles. His recent publications appear in the *Journal of Environment and Development*, *University of Denver Water Law Review*, and the *Journal of the Southwest*.

Joseph Nevins is Associate Professor in the Department of Earth Science and Geography at Vassar College, Poughkeepsie, NY, USA. His research interests include socio-territorial boundaries and mobility, violence and inequality, and political ecology.

Keith Pezzoli is Director of the Urban Studies and Planning Program at the University of California – San Diego, CA, USA, where he leads the Superfund Research Center's Community Engagement Core, with projects focused on socioecological challenges and health along the US–Mexico border. He founded The Global Action Research Center, a not-for-profit organisation that connects researchers to communities in pursuit of rooted community and resilient bioregional development.

Gudelia Rangel Gomez is currently in charge of the Office of the Executive Secretary of the US–Mexico Border Health Commission, Mexico Section. She is also Deputy Director General for Migrant Health of the Secretary of Health. From 2003 to 2007, she served as Director of the Department of Population Studies and later as General Director of Academic Affairs in the College of the Frontera Norte in Baja California, Mexico.

Christophe Sohn is Head of the Department of Urban Development and Mobility at the Centre for Population, Poverty and Public Policy Studies (CEPS) in Luxembourg. His current research, funded by the European Union, focuses on cross-border metropolitan integration processes and the changing significance of borders in Europe. He is the author of many articles in urban and border studies, and the editor of *Luxembourg: An Emerging Cross-Border Metropolitan Region* (2012).

Wilma Wooten is Public Health Officer and Director of Public Health Services for the County of San Diego Health and Human Services Agency. She oversees approximately 500 employees and a budget of over $110 million, serving a county of approximately 3.2 million residents. She is a board member for the California Conference of Local Health Officers (CCLHO), the Health Officers Association of California (HOAC), and the Public Health Accreditation Board (PHAB).

Globalisation, Place and Twenty-First-Century International Border Regions: An Introduction

LAWRENCE A. HERZOG

As we move deeper into the twenty-first century, the forces of globalisation continue to transform both the spaces around international borders and the social processes and political dynamics within and between these spaces. The future of international border regions and societies is now a critical area of scholarly inquiry.[1] The geographies of border regions have undergone a dramatic transformation over the last half century; nation-state boundaries grow ever more porous in many (though not all) areas of the planet. Global trade has become an accepted norm in business transactions almost everywhere. Coupled with the revolution in digital technology, the era of globalisation promises to continue to challenge old ideas with new approaches to understanding international boundaries and the regions they impact.

Scholarly debates about globalising borders began heating up in the 1980s and 1990s, when the first wave of the "deterritorialisation discourse" flourished. Where borders had previously been viewed as barriers, emerging phenomena such as global manufacturing and transnational trade, combined with seasonal or permanent cross-border labour migration, led to an outpouring of fresh debates and novel perspectives. Borders were viewed as becoming "softer" as global processes transcended them, bringing societies on either side into closer socio-economic contact. The new discourse on borders was highlighted by studies of cross-border change in North America and Europe.[2]

1. Border studies has become a major area of academic inquiry across the planet since the 1970s, with dozens of border academic and research centres in nations as far flung as Ireland, Russia, Denmark, the Netherlands, the UK, Mexico and the United States. There are major scholarly associations for border studies in both Europe (the Association of European Border Regions, formed in 1971) and North America (the Association of Borderland Studies, formed in 1976). These are mentioned in David Newman, "The Lines that Continue to Separate Us: Borders in a Borderless World", *Progress in Human Geography*, Vol. 10, No. 3 (2006), pp. 143–161.

2. Major works on the US–Mexico border during that era include Niles Hansen, *The Border Economy* (Austin, TX: University of Texas Press, 1981); John House, *Frontiers on the Rio Grande* (Oxford: Clarendon Press, 1982); Lawrence A. Herzog, *Where North Meets South: Cities, Space and Politics on the US–Mexico Border* (Austin, TX: University of Texas Press, 1990); Leslie Sklair, *Assembling for Development: The Maquila Industry in Mexico and the United States* (Boston, MA: Unwin Hyman, 1989); and Daniel Arreola and James Curtis, *The Mexican Border Cities* (Tucson, AZ: University of Arizona Press, 1993). Early work on European borders includes R. Strassoldo and G. Delli Zotti (eds.), *Cooperation and Conflict*

Frontier regions were no longer isolated and unproductive spaces at the margins of national life; they now had vital functions in a globalising world. From Western Europe to North America, some border regions served as "global conduits" for highly charged, multi-billion dollar import–export exchanges between nations, from transnational manufacturing and international tourism to cross-border commerce and other mutual exchanges. Some border zones evolved to become critical connectors—ports of entry for physical transshipment of the goods and services that feed the global economy. The structural dynamics, social composition, physical planning, urban design, transport/circulation planning and overall environmental management of these places represent some of the huge challenges facing these increasingly critical regions across the planet.

Examples from the US–Mexico border attest to the demographic and economic importance of frontier regions. Between 1980 and 2010, the populations of Mexican border states increased by over 50 per cent, from about 10.2 to 19.8 million inhabitants, while in that same period US border states grew from 41.8 million to 70.8 million, a gain of 59 per cent. This means that today, over 90 million people live in the US–Mexico border region states, with some 15 million now residing in the counties and Mexican municipalities physically fronting the boundary itself. These local borderland populations in the US and Mexico grew by nearly 20 per cent between 2000 and 2010. During the last several decades, the flourishing US–Mexican economy has seen bilateral trade grow from $100 billion at the signing of the North American Free Trade Agreement (NAFTA) in 1993 to $450 billion by 2011. Much of that trade flows literally through the land ports of the US–Mexican border, where the estimate in 2010 was $255 billion.[3] Since the 1960s, along the California–Mexico sector of the frontier, 35 million vehicles and 70 million passengers cross the border every year, along with merchandise valued at an average of over $30 billion. Those numbers are expected to double by the year 2020. Over 100,000 workers or more per week cross the border to work.[4]

A somewhat purist version of the deterritorialisation argument was the "borderless world" discourse, which posed the idea of a world where global trade and the flow of information render boundaries increasingly less necessary or relevant.[5] This position was challenged by political scientists, geographers, anthropologists and others. They viewed globalisation in a more nuanced fashion, arguing that borders were still being constructed in some parts of the world, while their role was diminishing in others.[6] The events of 9/11 led to yet another discourse, or "reterritorialisation", around the tightening of border controls and hardening of cross-border policy in response to threats of terrorism. This was especially severe along

---

in Border Areas (Milan: Franco Angeli Editore, 1982); J.M. Quintin, *European Cooperation in Frontier Regions* (Strasbourg: Council of Europe, 1973); Malcolm Anderson, "The Political Problems of Frontier Regions", *West European Politics*, Vol. 5, No. 4 (1982), pp. 1–17; and James Scott, "Transborder Cooperation, Regional Initiatives and Sovereignty Conflicts in the Upper Rhine Valley", *Publius: The Journal of Federalism*, Vol. 19 (Winter 1989), pp. 139–156.

3. All of these statistics are drawn or inferred from Christopher Wilson and Erik Lee (eds.), *The State of the Border Report* (Washington, DC: Wilson Center, 2013).

4. See Lawrence A. Herzog, *Global Crossroads: Planning and Infrastructure for the California–Baja California Border Region* (San Diego: Trans-border Institute, 2009).

5. For example, Kenichi Ohmae, *The Borderless World: Power and Strategy in the Interlinked Economy* (London: Harper Collins, 1990).

6. A good review of these literatures is found in Newman, *op. cit.*

the US–Mexico and US–Canadian borders.[7] Indeed, the push for homeland security has created uncertainty at the US–Mexican border. As a result, critical infrastructure remains unfunded or under-funded. Roads, new or upgraded rail transit lines, inspection facilities, new ports of entry, sewage treatment plants, air pollution monitoring systems and other vital projects have been delayed or cancelled for more than a decade. This is impacting the economies and ecologies of surrounding regions. The State of California, for example, is losing an estimated $6–8 billion and 50,000 jobs per year due to the perception or reality of excessive wait times at the border.[8]

We have, in the end, a set of two overarching theoretical discourses about borders and border regions. Scholars continue to explore the ways in which the boom in global trade, technology, cyberspace and transnational labour flows is bringing people together across borders. This approach, which speaks of the demise of the nineteenth-century view of borders as barriers, is sometimes termed "debordering." But, as mentioned, following the 9/11 tragedy in the US, a huge outpouring of work is being carried out on the shift towards "rebordering" and protecting the sovereignty of nation-states in an era of global terrorism. These two trends inevitably collide. Indeed, this journal published a special issue in 2013 on the subject of borders, security and politics. In that issue, attention was pointed towards the contradiction between the debordering trends in places like Australia, where the government is promoting economic integration with Asia while simultaneously implementing rebordering policies such as offshore detention centres for migrants and asylum seekers.[9]

Globalisation, Place and Border Regions in the New Century

While scholars debate whether "debordering" or "rebordering" defines global society in the twenty-first century, there is a third perspective that has often been missed by social scientists: the idea that border regions, over the last century, have become significant places in and of themselves, places that cry out for better understanding beyond the question of whether boundaries are "debordered" or "rebordered," and instead look to the future sustainability and wellbeing of the millions who live there. Indeed, by the first decades of the current century, scholars had begun exploring the nature of border regions themselves, for example through the lens of "cultural hybridity." A number of scholars emerged to explore innovations that result from the overlap of culture, economy and society that occurs along the US–Mexico border.[10] Indeed, one could even argue that border regions represent laboratories for the study of globalisation and the intermingling of cultures and societies in high density urbanising regions.[11]

7. Peter Andreas and Thomas J. Biersteker, *The Rebordering of North America: Integration and Exclusion in a New Security Context* (New York: Routledge, 2003).

8. San Diego Association of Governments (SANDAG), *Economic Impacts of Wait Times at the San Diego–Baja California Border*, Final Report (San Diego: SANDAG, 2006).

9. See Catarina Kinnvall, "Borders, Security and Global Governance", *Global Society*, Vol. 27, No. 3 (2013), pp. 261–266.

10. See Michael Dear and Gustavo Leclerc (eds.), *Postborder City: Cultural Spaces of Bajalta California* (New York and London: Routledge, 2003); Rosalea Monacella and Sue Anne Ware (eds.), *Fluctuating Borders* (Melbourne: RMIT University Press, 2007); Daniel Arreola (ed.), *Hispanic Spaces, Latino Places* (Austin, TX: University of Texas Press, 2004).

11. Lawrence A. Herzog, "Global Tijuana: The Seven Ecologies of the Border", in Dear and Leclerc, *op. cit.*, pp. 119–142.

Scholars should be concerned with the impacts of globalisation on border zones, or the ways in which those regions serve as prototypes for understanding the contradictions and dynamics of globalisation facing the rest of the planet. This special edition of *Global Society* brings together a number of those scholars. Our particular focus is the transformation of border regions as living spaces and unique places in a time of transition. Some scholars are calling for more "place-based" ecological integrity along borders, recognising the inherent holistic nature of border regions, no longer two separate nations or two separate societies but rather increasingly inter-connected transfrontier societies.[12]

In the past, when borders were marginal zones, far from major concentrations of economic activity and population clusters, one could understand the fact that so little attention was paid to them. But since at least the second half of the twentieth century, border regions have evolved to become important zones of wealth production in such sectors as global manufacturing, trade, specialised crafts and services. Today, millions live, work and interact in border regions as far reaching as Israel–Palestine, the former border enclave of China/Hong Kong/Macau, the Mexico–US and European border zones. While the articles in this special issue draw mainly from the US–Mexico border region, their approach is to deconstruct the impact of globalisation on international borders as dynamic socio-ecological constructions and concrete geographic places. The lessons from these articles are applicable across the planet.

All of the articles in this special issue speak to the ways in which border regions have become important places in their own right, spaces where people live and work, where corporations invest, and therefore spaces that need to be managed, despite the cross-national and global forces impinging upon them. The articles seek to explore a set of critical elements, including ecology, public health, cross-border cities, labour and, finally, security.

Ecology and International Borders

Border regions have their own complex and fragile ecosystems. Environmental preservation in borderland zones is complicated by three critical factors. First, bordering nations often have different national laws and institutional capacities when it comes to preserving nature. Second, border societies may also have different cultural views about the environment and how to sustain it. Third, the process of managing cross-border environments remains an institutional challenge for bordering nations across the planet, since there is no single political-administrative model for border ecological planning.

As Mumme points out in this volume, the border between Mexico and the US separates two distinct entities. On one side lies the United States, a highly industrialised nation with a well-institutionalised environmental movement that lacks representation in government and ends up relying on lobbying and litigation. On the other side sits Mexico, with a poorly institutionalised environmental movement, weak representation in government and a reliance on presidential discretion and administrative rules, and ultimately, a weak track record for ongoing environmental improvement. These differences have rendered the preservation of the environment in the booming US–Mexico border zone problematic, especially

12. Keith Pezzoli and his colleagues make this very point in their article in this special issue.

since the region experienced meteoric urban growth rates and a booming industrial assembly sector dating back to the 1970s.

The massive modernisation and urbanisation of the once marginal US–Mexico borderlands has left what the American Medical Association described as a "cesspool" of contamination, from toxic waste dumping sites, sewage contamination of critical water sources, and dangerously high levels of air pollution. Millions of citizens who now live in northern Mexico and the south-western United States are at risk. Taking on this deeply vulnerable environmental crisis, Mumme analyses the political-institutional responses following the North American Free Trade Agreement in the early 1990s. More than two decades after this massive "debordering" policy shift, Mumme argues that the two nations have not succeeded in confronting the big environmental threats facing citizens. The planning agency created by the NAFTA agreement, the Border Environmental Cooperation Commission (BECC), and its funding partner, the National Development Bank (NADB), have spent several billion dollars on infrastructure, but gradually funds have not been replenished, while conservative governments of the first decades of the new century in both nations ushered in an era of diminishing commitment to environmental initiatives. This reversal of commitment to protecting nature in the borderlands is a stunning defeat for both nations. It brings to light the problem that, given the uncertainties of binational policy-making, protecting nature along international boundaries may be difficult during the remainder of the twenty-first century.

Public Health across Boundaries: The Case for a Bioregional Approach

A second important challenge to our thinking about international borders lies in the question of how we conceptualise border regions in terms of citizen well-being. As Pezzoli and his colleagues point out in their article, national boundaries are generally antithetical to the ecological arrangement of the planet, since they often literally cut across mountain chains, divide river basins and otherwise ignore nature. This becomes increasingly problematic as these regions have become more densely populated and developed more diverse economies, including manufacturing and commerce, which involve the construction of infrastructure that can contaminate the ecosystem. The article by Pezzoli and his co-writers makes this clear, pointing to the example of the California–Baja California case of the Mexicali-Calexico urbanised region, where toxic pesticides from large-scale, intensive agriculture and chemical runoff from industrial assembly plants are combining to seriously contaminate the region's watershed, which runs from the New River to the Salton Sea. This has led to documented cancer clusters.

Pezzoli's research team raises the question of bioregional health in cross-border regions. They argue that the only way to manage contemporary global public health challenges, like the spread of diseases such as HIV, SARS, Avian flu or dengue fever, is by framing the problem in a bioregional framework. This acknowledges that cross-border outbreaks of disease require early warning systems and other institutional structures that connect to the bioregion. The University of California research team has crafted an innovative policy initiative called One Bioregion One Health (OBOH). This institutional concept moves away from both "metrocentric" (over-emphasis on the city) and "anthropocentric" (over-emphasis on humans) ways of thinking, towards an approach that is respectful of the city/

countryside connection (e.g. food and natural components in the hinterland intimately connected to urban sustainability), as well as the human/animal connection (e.g. preservation of wildlife, sustainability of animals within the animal/human food chain).

Cross-Border Metropolitan Regions

As international border regions have shifted from being marginal and isolated to places where urbanisation, industrialisation and economic development are occurring, we must begin to conceptualise cross-border urbanisation. Herzog and Sohn, in their article in this volume, speak to the emergence of the "transfrontier metropolis," and both the theoretical and practical urban planning implications of these twenty-first-century spaces. Conceptually, they revisit the ideas of "debordering" and "rebordering," exploring their applicability to the case of cross-border urban regions. They view debordering through the act of constructing built environments and planning approaches that are cross-border in nature. But they also recognise that in a globalising world there are new dangers, from drug smuggling to terrorism, and therefore governments and interest groups are seeking greater securitisation and "rebordering," especially in urban areas which are more vulnerable due to higher-density concentrations of people.

Herzog and Sohn argue that, while these may seem dialectic and in opposition, they can also be viewed simply as part of a general scheme of "bordering" in places, which is dynamic, ever-changing and sometimes contradictory in urbanised boundary zones. They go on to recognise the ways in which debordering can be seen as either a threat or a resource, and rebordering as an obstacle or a working shield. By tracking the recent histories of US–Mexico (San Diego–Tijuana) and Europe (Geneva–French metropolis) metropolitan cases, they illustrate how border regions pass through different historic eras, where debordering and rebordering dynamics play out, are negotiated and renegotiated, as cities and nations cope with the challenges of border region urbanisation.

Workers

International border regions have long been thought of as "pass-through" zones for migrant workers heading to employment destinations in the interiors of nation-states. However, as border regions grew and sustained their own economies and spawned cities of significant size in some parts of the world, workers crossed and remained in the border region itself. This has been well documented in the case of the US–Mexico border region, but is also true in other parts of the world, notably Europe. Workers represent a significant segment in the daily life of border regions.

Of course, over time, changes in national immigration policy have an impact on workers in the border region. Indeed, sometimes the border region has been targeted by national governments to symbolically enforce new policies, or changes in policy. That is precisely the concern taken by Joseph Nevins in his article for this special issue. Nevins confronts the ongoing question of human rights for cross-border immigrants in the twenty-first century. He argues that US immigration policy has "hardened," in line with the aforementioned "rebordering" trend connected with the idea of greater territorial control in an era of "homeland security." He uses the case of a US immigration authority raid on a restaurant in San Diego, California, and the subsequent deportation of workers who did not have proper documentation, as an example of a trend where the federal government is trying to coerce employers and business owners into cooperating with government-led policing of workplaces, to, in Nevin's view, ultimately "cleanse" them of unauthorised workers.

Nevins' article raises a number of critical questions for international border regions. If cross-border workers supply much-needed labour for global economic activities in urbanising border regions, what are the trade-offs between "debordering" policies that facilitate cross-border laboor migration, on the one hand, and "rebordering" policies that curtail or contain those worker movements, on the other? And to what extent does this grey area of policy-making render the quality of life of workers more precarious, and thus become a concern for the defence of their human rights? Should governments be in the business of policing workers or protecting their rights?

Borders and Security

In the end, the dialectic between debordering and rebordering becomes a paradox for life along the border. In a global era, how can nations like Mexico and the United States, or the members of the European Community, engage in cross-border trade and build globally strong economic relations while constructing fences and other security infrastructure designed to curtail movement and filter out flows amidst the threats of terrorism, violence, drug smuggling or illegal immigration? Paul Ashby's article in this volume speaks directly to this paradox for the case of the United States and Mexico, and the border regions in which millions reside.

If border regions are, indeed, independent, thriving ecosystems, places with their own unique histories, culture and ecology, is the threat of overzealous securitisation also a threat to their ability to preserve their environment and maintain both quality of life and their newly thriving identities? To what extent might the homeland security paradigm of fences, surveillance and more border patrol agents in the field along the US–Mexico border compromise the $500 billion cross-border trade economy? And how can local governments protect their interests in the midst of federally approved massive spending for border security infrastructure? Will all of this security apparatus eventually curtail border crossings, and thus diminish the US–Mexico border economy, and therefore the well-being of millions who now make the border region(s) their home?

Trade and Environmental Protection along the United States–Mexico Border

STEPHEN P. MUMME

This article examines environmental protection along the US–Mexico border since the North American Free Trade Agreement (NAFTA) took effect in January 1994. It first reviews the general and border-specific neoliberal arguments positing a favourable relationship between trade agreements and environmental protection. It then reviews the trajectory of environmental policy along the border, focusing on the principal institutions and programmes developed pursuant to NAFTA. The article shows that while NAFTA-derived environmental agencies and programmes have partially mitigated the adverse environmental impact of trade at the border, they have not kept pace with these developments, nor do they compensate for trade-related national security policies that hinder the implementation of environmental protection at the border.

Introduction

The region straddling the US border with Mexico is well situated on the cutting edge of globalisation. If globalisation is taken to mean the process "of societal transformation that encompasses ... growth in trade, investment, travel, computer networking, and transboundary pollution", it is hard to escape its imprint on a border region that has been a prominent locale for globalising practices since those practices were embraced as a cornerstone of US foreign policy at the end of World War II.[1] As early as 1965, a bilateral focus on the US–Mexico border area as a platform for assembly for export operations (under the auspices of the well-known Border Industrialisation Program [BIP]), initiated a process of rapid industrialisation that continues unabated today.[2] Many of the manufacturing techniques and export practices now found across the globe were pioneered in this region, as well as their negative externalities in the form of social and environmental degradation and persistent economic dependency. By the mid-1970s, not much more than a decade after the BIP was rolled out, the environmental problems associated with this mode of development were clearly apparent. By 1983, mounting problems, including the transboundary spillover of rapid urbanisation, led the two countries to their first binational agreement addressing the mitigation of

1. Lawrence A. Herzog, *Where North Meets South: Cities, Space, and Politics on the US–Mexico Border* (Austin, TX: Center for Mexican Studies, University of Texas, 1990), pp. 60–62.

2. Leslie Sklair, *Assembling for Development* (updated edn.) (La Jolla, CA: Center for US–Mexican Studies, 1993), pp. 27–31.

environmental problems along the border. A decade later, as the newly minted North American Free Trade Agreement (NAFTA) spurred these globalising trends, new environmental agreements were struck to mitigate their adverse effects.

This article examines the trajectory of environmental protection along the US–Mexico border since NAFTA entered into force. It begins with a brief review of the NAFTA debate and the agreements it spawned to protect the border environment. It then reports on the implementation and principal achievements of these agreements since 1994. These achievements are important and have partially buffered the border environment from the impact of globalisation, yet fall well short of the hopes and expectations of the border environmental community and the needs of border communities. The conclusion points to the enduring environmental stresses associated with globalisation along the border, the imperative of adopting a more strategic and comprehensive approach to environmental protection, and the need to need reinvigorate and strengthen federal commitments to environmental protection along the border.

Globalisation, the Environment and NAFTA

Advocates for the diffusion of neoliberal economic reforms make the case that globalisation over the long term is beneficial for environmental protection. This argument is supported by the environmental Kusnet's curve that shows a strong positive correlation between quantitative indicators of economic development and the abatement of certain forms of industrial pollution beyond a certain threshold of development, pegged at around USD 5,000 per capita income.[3] Proponents of globalisation also point to the correlation between education and awareness of environmental values in structuring demand for environmental protection in democratising countries. They argue that market liberalisation attracts international investment, generating employment, economic growth and resources for environmental improvement, and stimulating public demand for greater regulation of environmental abuses. Some also argue that because globalisation is associated with multilateral trade regulation and diffusion of the business rule of law, such developments are sure to strengthen and harmonise administrative practices meant to limit commercial advantages arising from lax environmental regulations.

A flaw in this line of reasoning is its depreciation of the structural barriers of economic asymmetry and differentials in political power within and among nations that interfere with the distribution of market benefits. Even the most dogmatic trade religionists admit that liberalised trade aggravates economic differences, certainly in the short run, that trade liberalisation is inherently redistributive, that it shifts wealth creation from low skills to high skills venues, and that its benefits normally flow to those best positioned to engage the new

3. Kevin P. Gallagher, "Mexico–United States: The Environmental Costs of Trade-Led Growth", in Liane Schalatek (ed.), *Globalization and the Environment: Lessons from the Americas* (Washington, DC: Working Group on Development and Environment in the Americas, The Heinrich Boll Foundation North America, 2004), pp. 25–28; David Stern, Michael Common and Edward Barbier, "Economic Growth and Environmental Degradation: The Environmental Kuznets Curve and Sustainability", *World Development*, Vol. 24 (1996), pp. 1151–1160; Neil Carter, *The Politics of the Environment*, 2nd edn. (Cambridge: Cambridge University Press, 2007).

rules. Eventually, of course, the benefits of growth are supposed to dribble down to the less fortunate—witness *The Economist* trumpeting the "end of poverty," attributing reduction of the direst form of global poverty to free trade and citing China as evidence of trade's virtues.[4] Such sanguinity conveniently overlooks persistent and deepening sweatshop conditions in China and throughout the developing world and lowballs corporate resistance to state-led socio-economic and environmental improvements.[5]

The political corollary of this "it gets worse before it gets better, but it will get better" perspective on trade accords is less well developed. Liberal international relations scholars see free markets as fundamental in sustaining cooperative behaviour in the global community and thus contributing to the rise of multilateral environmental institutions.[6] Comparative government scholars tend to argue that, other things being equal, trade-driven economic expansion strengthens state power and bourgeoisie authority in government, contributing to the rise of liberal democracies.[7] Many political scientists accept one version or another of Robert Dahl's thesis that economic liberalisation is conducive to the emergence of polyarchical modes of governance in which corporate economic interests play a leading political role.[8] Elinor Ostrom, for example, is well known for her advocacy of economic rationality and polycentric governance[9]—another way of arguing that political pluralism is good for democracy and, by extension, environmental governance.

This benign view of a favourable relationship between market economies, democracy and environmental protection is not without critics. While accepting that democracy is generally good for the environment, ecological modernisation theorists argue that state support for environmental values is contingent on environmentalists' ability to successfully link environmental values to core liberal state imperatives of economic growth and political legitimation.[10] However, as John Drysek et al. observe, environmentalists in leading liberal democracies have fallen well short of achieving this goal.[11] State commitment to a programme of ecological modernisation (or sustainable development) varies considerably across countries depending on the representation of environmental interests in government and the strength of national environmental movements.

The impact of trade on ecological modernisation thus depends substantially on the character of the regimes engaged in a trading relationship. The close nexus between economic and political power in liberal democracies means these

---

4. *The Economist*, "Towards the End of Poverty", 1–7 June 2013, p. 11.

5. War on Want, "Sweatshops in China", available: <http://www.waronwant.org/overseas-work/sweatshops-and-plantations/china-sweatshops>.

6. Gabriela Kutting, *Globalization and the Environment* (New York: SUNY Press, 2004), pp. 12–17.

7. A short list of prominent scholars making this point would include Barrington Moore, Jr., *Social Origins of Dictatorship and Democracy* (Boston, MA: Beacon Press, 1966); Theda Skocpol, *States and Social Revolutions* (Cambridge: Cambridge University Press, 1979); Douglass C. North, *Structure and Change in Economic History* (New York: Norton, 1981).

8. Robert A. Dahl, *Polyarchy* (New Haven, CT: Yale University Press, 1971).

9. Elinor E. Ostrom, *Governing the Commons* (Cambridge: Cambridge University Press, 1990; and "Polycentric Systems for Coping with Collective Action and Global Environmental Change", *Global Environmental Change*, Vol. 20 (2010), pp. 550–557.

10. John Drysek et al., *Green States and Social Movements* (New York: Oxford University Press, 2003), p. 164.

11. *Ibid.*, p. 191.

agreements are likely to sustain and strengthen market resistance to environmental regulation, absent a strong environmental movement and concerted state intervention to prevent this result. This is likely to occur even when states officially subscribe to multilateral environmental agreements or, as with NAFTA, trade liberalisation comes draped in new inclusionary language embracing sustainable development and acknowledging the importance of social and environmental values. In the case of the US–Mexico border, we have one state, highly industrialised, with a well-institutionalised environmental movement but one that lacks direct representation in government and relies on lobbying and litigation for influence, and another state, rapidly industrialising and trade dependent on its neighbour, with a poorly institutionalised environmental movement and weak green representation in government, relying on presidential discretion, administrative rules and weak administrative capacity for environmental improvement.

An ecological modernisation perspective thus suggests that intensified international trade should logically amplify regional environmental stresses considering the economic and political asymmetries found along the US–Mexico border and considering the moderate to weak influence of environmentalists on state policy in these neighbouring countries. This argument was energetically advanced by environmental critics of the NAFTA initiative,[12] resulting in side agreements meant to mitigate adverse trade effects on the border environment. The economic and political asymmetry in environmental capacity between the two countries meant the burden of harnessing trade to the environment fell heavily on the United States. The degree of mitigation would thus depend on new and strengthened environmental institutions, strengthened and sustained government investment in environmental protection, and increased opportunities for public voice in border area environmental management. NAFTA's impact on ecological modernisation must be evaluated in these terms.

NAFTA's Border Challenge

Free trade's environmental challenge is acutely visible along the US–Mexico border where profound economic asymmetry historically cohabits with a certain degree of socio-economic interdependence along a boundary nearly 2,000 miles long. As Leslie Sklair observes, the emergence of Mexico's northern border region as an assembly-for-export platform after 1960 meant this region was effectively a free trade zone 30 years prior to NAFTA, which then deepened and broadened the zone.[13] Trade-led growth boosted Mexican border cities, producing well over a million jobs by the year 2000, but wages and working conditions remained stagnant. The quality of life conducive to environmental betterment failed to materialise. What did materialise was the contaminating spillover of poorly regulated industries.

In the policy debate preceding NAFTA approval, many of the neoliberal arguments were advanced to rebut the criticisms of environmentalists concerned with NAFTA's potentially adverse impacts on environmental conditions in the border

12. John J. Audley, *Green Politics and Global Trade: NAFTA and the Future of Environmental Politics* (Washington, DC: Georgetown University Press, 1997).

13. Sklair, *op. cit.*, pp. 27–31.

region. For example, a 1991 review of NAFTA's likely environmental effects by the Office of the US Trade Representative argued:

> Through its income and growth effects, the NAFTA should have a significant positive effect on the environment in the US Mexico border region, in Mexico as a nation, and serve as an example to all the world as to how two neighboring countries can address trade and environmental issues in parallel, mutually enforcing fashion.[14]

The same report touted the likely new investments in environmentally relevant infrastructure that would surely be an outcome of the trade agreement.[15] Prominent trade economists agreed.[16]

At the time of the NAFTA debates, many environmentalists were underwhelmed by these arguments.[17] They pointed to the border's chronic deficit in environmental infrastructure, disparities in standards and regulatory practices between the two countries, and the extraordinary stresses that accelerated trade and investment would impose on the human and natural environment in the border area. In response to environmental criticism, in 1992 a new presidential-congressional advisory board on US–Mexico border environmental issues was established by the US Congress.[18] In early 1992, the US and Mexican governments rolled out a new environmental plan, the Integrated Border Environmental Plan (IBEP), highlighting border area environmental initiatives already underway and promising greater attention to sustainable development and environmental cooperation along the border.[19] These measures were widely received in the environmental community as public relations initiatives intended to soften up environmentalists and blunt criticism of the trade deal. Faced with opposition from environmentalists and labour, the governments agreed to negotiate separate side agreements that addressed these concerns.

By the time the ink was dry on the NAFTA agreement, environmentalists had wrung three important environmental commitments from the governments. The first, the North American Agreement on Environmental Cooperation (NAAEC),

---

14. Office of the United States Trade Representative (USTR), *Draft: Review of US–Mexican Environmental Issues* (Washington, DC: Interagency Task Force Coordinated by the Office of the US Trade Representative, 1991), pp. 190–191; Steven Shrybman, "Trading Away the Environment", in Ricardo Grinspun and Maxwell A. Cameron (eds.), *The Political Economy of North American Free Trade* (New York: St. Martin's Press, 1993), p. 283.

15. Office of the USTR, *op. cit.*, p. 191.

16. Jagdish Bhagwati, "Trade and the Environment: The False Conflict?", in Durwood Zaelke, Paul Orbuch and Robert F. Housman (eds.), *Trade and the Environment* (Washington, DC: Island Press, 1993), pp. 159–190.

17. Michael Gregory, "Environment, Sustainable Development, Public Participation, and the NAFTA: A Retrospective", *Journal of Environmental Law and Litigation*, Vol. 7 (1992), pp. 102–104; Tom Barry and Beth Sims, *The Challenge of Cross-Border Environmentalism: The US–Mexico Case* (Albuquerque: Resource Center Press, 1994), p. 97.

18. The Good Neighbor Environmental Board (GNEB) was authorised by the Enterprise for the Americas Initiative Act of 1992 (7 US Code Section 5404). It was fully established and operational in 1994. See *First Annual Report of the Good Neighbor Environmental Board* (Washington, DC: Environmental Protection Agency [EPA], GNEB, October 1995), p. 2, available: <http://www.epa.gov/ocem/gneb/gneb1streport/gneb_1st_report.pdf>.

19. Environmental Protection Agency, *Integrated Environmental Plan for the Mexican–US Border Area, 1992–1994* (Washington, DC: EPA, A92-171.toc, 1992).

was a trinational agreement aimed at supporting environmental regulation and strengthening cooperation on environmental issues in the North American region.[20] The second, a binational agreement between the United States and Mexico, established a Border Environment Cooperation Commission (BECC) and North American Development Bank (NADB) in support of environmental investment and projects in the border area.[21] The third, also binational, was to build on the 1992–1994 IBEP and redouble efforts to improve binational environmental protection under the auspices of the 1983 US–Mexico Agreement to Cooperate for the Improvement of the Border Environment (labelled the La Paz Agreement for the port city on Mexico's Baja peninsula where the pact was signed).[22] These achievements were unprecedented and were praised for raising the border region's profile on the binational policy agenda. The question of their sufficiency as policy buffers to trade-generated environmental stresses remained open, however.

To appreciate the challenge these new policies and institutions confronted at the time NAFTA was struck, it is useful to briefly describe the prevailing economic and environmental conditions along the international boundary at the time. By 1990, the *maquiladora* boom had produced a 31 per cent increase in urban population in Mexico's border cities over levels found in 1970.[23] Tijuana's population had grown to 992,000 in 1995 from 461,000 in 1980; Cd. Juarez mushroomed to 1,012,000 from 567,000 in the same period.[24] Other Mexican border cities had seen similar population growth. The number of *maquiladoras* located along the border had grown from 120 in 1970 to 1,477 in 1990.[25] While the Mexican border region's sewage infrastructure coverage in 1990 exceeded the national average,[26] it lagged well below nearly blanket coverage on the US side of the boundary[27] and actual treatment capacity served just 34 per cent of Mexico's border population.[28] Air quality had deteriorated in major metropolitan areas and clandestine dumpsites for hazardous and toxic waste proliferated. Valuable wetlands like the internationally important Tijuana River estuary were threatened by sewage, the

20. North American Agreement for Environmental Cooperation (1993), available: <http://www.cec.org/Page.asp?PageID=1226&SiteNodeID=567>.

21. "Agreement Concerning the Establishment of a Border Environment Cooperation Commission and a North American Development Bank", *International Legal Materials*, Vol. 32 (1993), p. 1545.

22. "Agreement between the United States of America and the United Mexican States on Cooperation for the Protection and Improvement of the Environment in the Border Area", La Paz, Baja California Sur (14 August 1983), US-Mex, TIAS No. 10827.

23. Joan Anderson and James Gerber, *Fifty Years of Change on the US–Mexican Border* (Austin, TX: University of Texas Press, 2008), p. 103.

24. James Peach and James Williams, "Population and Economic Dynamics on the US–Mexican Border: Past, Present, and Future Trends", in Paul Ganster (ed.), *The US–Mexican Border Environment: Road Map to a Sustainable 2020* (San Diego, CA: Southwest Center for Environmental Research and Policy, Monograph Series No. l, San Diego State University Press, 2000), p. 60.

25. Elwynn Stoddard, *Maquila: Assembly Plants in Northern Mexico* (El Paso: Texas Western Press, 1987), p. 24; David E. Lorey, *United States–Mexico Border Statistics since 1900* (Los Angeles, CA: University of California at Los Angeles, Latin American Center Publications, 1993), p. 99.

26. Lorey, *op. cit.*, p. 110.

27. *Ibid.*, p. 99; Office of the USTR, *op. cit.*, p. 102.

28. General Accounting Office (GAO), *International Environment: Environmental Infrastructure Needs in the US–Mexican Border Region Remain Unmet* (Washington, DC: GAO/RCED-96-179, July 1996), pp. 7–8. The distinction here is between the percentage of occupied homes with drainage facilities and the percentage of the total population served by wastewater treatment facilities.

by-product of industrialisation and urban sprawl. Sewage and pesticides contaminated much of the Rio Grande, provoking hazards warnings in urbanised zones on the river.[29] Reports described an environmental infrastructure deficit on the order of USD 8–10 billion.[30] It is small wonder that the American Medical Association described the border as a "cesspool" of contamination in 1990.[31] This was the state of affairs after a decade of environmental cooperation under the La Paz Agreement prior to NAFTA.

Border Environmental Policy since NAFTA: CEC, BECC and the La Paz Agreement Programmes

These conditions notwithstanding, or perhaps because of them, the advent of the new policies and institutions was received with a degree of anticipation and optimism along the border. Now, nearly two decades on, we can track the trajectory of these policy reforms and gain a better understanding of what they actually accomplished. While some environmental policy gains are evident along the border, it is also clear that these achievements have fallen well short of their promise and well short of an active agenda of environmental modernisation. This can be seen with respect to each of the mentioned agreements and their consequences along the border.

The Commission for Environmental Cooperation

Of the various NAFTA-related environmental programmes that were meant to mitigate the impact of accelerated economic integration along the border, the North American Agreement on Environmental Cooperation was the most heralded. As far as the border environment is concerned it is also the most disappointing.

NAAEC was conceived as a broad, near comprehensive environmental agreement that would hold the governments accountable for the implementation of domestic environmental laws and stimulate greater international cooperation among the parties in support of environmental protection and the conservation of natural resources. The NAAEC and its institutional arm, the Commission for Environmental Cooperation (CEC), were tasked with a trans-continental mission, protecting North American ecosystems and centring attention on environmental issues of North American scope. From the beginning the CEC had a limited interest in strictly binational environmental problems. Even so, many environmentalists had higher expectations for its impact on the border than it delivered.

29. Alan D. Hecht, Patrick Whelan and Sarah Sowell, "Sustainable Development on the US–Mexican Border: Past Lessons, Present Efforts, Future Possibilities", in Paul Ganster (ed.), *The US–Mexican Border Environment. Economy and Environment for a Sustainable Border Region: Now and in 2020* (San Diego, CA: Southwest Center for Environmental Research and Policy, Monograph Series No. 3, San Diego State University Press, 2002), p. 15.

30. D. Rick Van Schoik, "A Verification and Meta-Analysis of Past Border Environmental Infrastructure Needs Assessments", in Ganster, *The US–Mexican Border Environment. Economy and Environment for a Sustainable Border Region, op. cit.*, pp. 155–156.

31. American Medical Association, "A Permanent US–Mexico Border Health Commission", *Journal of the American Medical Association*, No. 263 (1990), pp. 3319–3321.

In general, the CEC effort can be analysed in two parts. The first part centres on its record in the area of inquiries and investigations, both with respect to so-called citizen-initiated investigations of government non-compliance with existing environmental law and secretariat-initiated investigations for the purpose of spot-lighting important environmental issues of regional importance. The second part deals with its various programmes advancing environmental cooperation among the North American nations.

The CEC's record with inquiries and investigations is mixed overall and certainly where the border is concerned. From its inception through to December 2012 the Commission had undertaken 81 citizen-initiated investigations based on citizen allegations of governmental non-compliance with legislated environmental norms.[32] Under the procedure, citizen appeals must first pass rigorous review of allegations by the Secretariat, including proof that appellants have first exhausted domestic legal and administrative remedies before approaching the CEC.[33] If the appeal passes muster, the Secretariat may then recommend a factual investigation for the approval of the parties (the Commission). At least two of the three nations must approve before a "factual record" investigation is launched. When completed, two of the three nations must also approve any public release of the information and recommendations gleaned from the effort. In short, the practical impediments to gaining a factual investigation are daunting. Even so, by providing a means for civil society to prod the governments to strengthen environmental enforcement, this procedure has benefitted the border community.

Since 1994, a total of 40 citizen submissions have been submitted for CEC consideration from Mexico and another 10 allegations submitted from the United States. Of these, 10 of the Mexican submissions and three of the US submissions were generated from border states. Most of these border state submissions emanated from the interior of these states—just three of the Mexican submissions and one of the US submissions could properly be described as located in the border region. Of these four submissions, two generated factual records, one, in 2000, involving the notorious case of Metales y Derivados, a lead battery recycling plant in Tijuana, Baja California and the other, in 2002, a case of untreated waste-water discharged to the Rio Magdalena in Sonora.[34] In the case of Metales y Derivados, the CEC investigation contributed to plant closure and clean-up; in the Rio Magdalena case, its investigation highlighted various failures to adequately enforce federal water quality norms applicable to the alleged violation with limited results. Although most observers agree that the factual investigations have been useful when they have occurred,[35] the small number of these cases is indicative of the CEC's limited reach in the border area. It is notable that no factual investigations

32. Commission for Environmental Cooperation, *Registry of Submissions* (Montreal, Quebec, 2013), available: <http://www.cec.org/Page.asp?PageID=751&SiteNodeID=250>.

33. Procedures for citizen submissions are detailed in: *Citizen Submissions on Enforcement Matters, North American Environmental Law and Policy, No. 26* (Montreal, Quebec: Commission for Environmental Cooperation, 2008).

34. Commission for Environmental Cooperation, *Metales y Derivados, Final Factual Record*, SEM-98-007 (2001), available: <http://www.cec.org/Storage/84/7955_98-7-FFR-e.pdf>; Commission for Environmental Cooperation, *Factual Record Río Magdalena Submission*, SEM-97-002 (2003), available: <http://www.cec.org/Storage/67/6076_97-2-FFR_en.pdf>.

35. Joseph Dimento and Pamela M. Doughman, "Soft Teeth in the Back of the Mouth: The NAFTA Environmental Side Agreement Implemented", *The Georgetown International Environmental Law Review*, Vol. 10, No. 3 (1998), p. 695; David L. Markell, "The CEC Citizen Submission Process: On or Off

have been mounted in more than a decade in a region known for its many environmental problems.

The Secretariat's Article 13 investigations afford an opportunity to spotlight important issues concerning environmental policy and several of these investigations have been mounted in the border area. Since 1994, the CEC's Secretariat has conducted eight such special investigations. Two of these investigations have focused on the border area. One of the earliest such investigations, *Ribbon of Life*, focused on the conservation of the San Pedro River watershed that spans Arizona's border with Sonora.[36] This investigation, mounted in 1998, is the catalyst for an ongoing binational cooperative endeavour aimed at protecting the San Pedro's water resources and surrounding ecosystem. In 2012, another investigation, this one focused on the spent lead-acid battery recycling trade in North America—inspired by the problems associated with Metales y Derivados, among others—aims to strengthen regulations and improve practices associated with the reprocessing of batteries, most of which is done in Mexican border cities.[37] The CEC's Article 13 investigations have certainly addressed important border issues, drawing much needed public attention to particular problems, but as with the Article 14 citizen-initiated investigations, the small number of these studies limits the Commission's impact on the border area.

The CEC's work programme is in various aspects relevant to the border area even though the border per se is seldom singled out for special attention. The CEC's charter specifically references "transboundary activities" for consideration in its work programme but by 1998 the Secretariat had eliminated this area of work from its active portfolio, partly to avoid duplication of other environmental and conservation programmes being undertaken by the governments and to avoid unnecessary conflicts with domestic and binational agencies. An early programme to provide small seed grants to environmental non-governmental organisations (NGOs) along the border, the North American Fund for Environmental Cooperation, was also abandoned by 2002.

While the CEC is officially North American in scope, a number of its programmes, particularly those involving conservation and toxic substances, do tend to target or favourably impact the border region. The CEC's current work programme is divided into three broad priority areas: 1. Healthy Communities and Ecosystems; 2. Climate Change and Low-Carbon Economy; and 3. Greening the Economy in North America.[38] Of the 16 projects spread across these priority areas of work, one, the Big Bend–Rio Bravo Collaboration for Landscape Conservation/North American Invasive Species Network, directly targets the border region.[39] Other programmes including the North American Grasslands Initiative,

Course?", in David L. Markell and John H. Knox (eds.), *Greening NAFTA: The North American Commission for Environmental Cooperation* (Palo Alto, CA: Stanford University Press, 2003), pp. 790–791.

36. Commission for Environmental Cooperation, *Ribbon of Life. An Agenda for Preserving Transboundary Migratory Bird Habitat on the Upper San Pedro River* (1999), available: <http://www.cec.org/Storage/31/2263_Ribbon-engl_EN.pdf>.

37. Commission for Environmental Cooperation, *Final Draft Report. Hazardous Trade: An Examination of US Generated Spent Lead-Acid Battery Exports and Secondary Lead Recycling in Mexico, the United States, and Canada* (Montreal, Quebec: Commission for Environmental Cooperation, 2012).

38. Commission for Environmental Cooperation, *Operational Plan of the Commission for Environmental Cooperation 2013–2014*, available: <http://www.cec.org/Storage/156/18291_CEC_OP_Plan_and_Budget_22jan14_en.pdf>.

39. *Ibid.*

the Pollutant Release and Transfer Tracking Project, the Risk Reduction Strategies to Reduce the Exposure to Chemicals of Mutual Concern Project, the Environmental Monitoring and Assessment of Chemicals of Mutual Concern Project, the Environmental Law Enforcement Enhancement Project, and a project focused on the Sound Management of Electronic Wastes in North America have some indirect benefits for the border region.[40] The CEC has also spotlighted endangered and threatened species in the border region that are deemed vital for the preservation of North American ecosystems through its Species of Common Concern initiative.[41] In general, the CEC has used its offices to partner with other domestic agencies of the three governments to draw attention to and raise awareness of environmental problems. It has also performed useful information and legitimation functions by disseminating environmental data and supporting public participation in environmental decision making throughout the North American zone.

For all its efforts, however, the CEC has received slight attention from its member governments, who seem to regard it as little more than window dressing for their limited interest in transboundary environmental cooperation. The Commission's budget remains the same as it was in 1994 (USD 9 million), despite inflation, compelling the Secretariat to scale back programmes over the past decade.[42] Indeed, apart from the several inquiries and investigations mentioned above and a few border-targeted programmes, it is difficult to discern the CEC's impact on the border environment. Along the border, environmentalists had certainly hoped for more.

The Border Environmental Cooperation Commission

Of the several border-related environmental initiatives that accompanied NAFTA, the Border Environment Cooperation Commission (BECC) and its financial partner, the North American Development Bank (NADB), have arguably been the most consequential, precisely because these programmes came with funding and have over time been better supported by the governments. The BECC, as conceived in 1993, was intended to directly address the environmental infrastructure deficit identified in the NAFTA debates. Designed as a distinctly binational agency located in Cd. Juarez, Chihuahua, BECC was to technically assist, receive, assess and authorise desirable environmental projects for the border area, employing sustainable development criteria in its project approval process.[43] Initially, at least, it was to be especially representative of border and environmental

40. *Ibid.*

41. Stephen P. Mumme, Donna Lybecker, Osiris Gaona and Carlos Monterola, "The Commission for Environmental Cooperation and Transboundary Conservation across the US–Mexico Border", in L. Lopez-Hoffman, E. McGovern, R. Varady and K. Flessa (eds.), *Conservation of Shared Environments: Learning from the United States and Mexico* (Tucson, AZ: University of Arizona Press, 2009), pp. 261–278.

42. Stephen P. Mumme and Donna Lybecker, "The Commission for Environmental Cooperation as a Model for Promoting Sustainable Development in the Americas", *International Journal of Sustainable Society*, Vol. 3, No. 2 (2011), pp. 151–173.

43. Mark Spalding, "Addressing Border Environmental Problems Now and in the Future: Border XXI and Related Efforts", in Ganster, *The US–Mexican Border Environment: Road Map to a Sustainable 2020, op. cit.*, pp. 124–125.

constituencies, open to public participation at both the operational and project levels, and transparent in its decision-making procedures.[44] At the outset, border environmentalists had high hopes for BECC.

Now, after nearly two decades, it can be said that BECC has not lived up to the more ambitious expectations of the environmental community, although it is also true that it has become architecturally vital for environmental infrastructure development in the border area. As of December 2010, BECC had approved more than 175 projects on either side of the international boundary and with NADB's assistance directed nearly USD 4 billion to a wide range of projects, most of these focused on potable water and sanitation provision but including sanitary landfills, road paving, constructed wetlands, water conservation and, more recently, renewable energy projects enabling better compliance with water treaty provisions along the border.[45] The sum of funding and projects has fallen well short of estimated needs but has nevertheless realised important improvements in certain areas of the border environment agenda, notably wastewater treatment and potable water provision. At least one study finds that BECC's unique binational design has also helped to bridge the administrative and governance barriers that complicate binational cooperation for environmental improvement along the border.[46]

BECC's jurisdiction, oversight and procedures have also altered since its inception. Originally, BECC's jurisdiction was administratively defined as 100 km north and south of the international line, following the guidelines set by the 1983 La Paz Agreement. In 2001, the board approved the extension of the Commission's functional mandate to environmental infrastructure projects beyond water provision, sewage and wastewater projects. These changes enhanced BECC's portfolio of projects and its geographical impact.[47] Shortly after, the BECC's board of directors agreed to extend jurisdiction another 200 km further into Mexico, enabling BECC and NADB to address a wider range of needs along the border. In 2004, hoping to streamline project development, the governments revised the BECC-NABD charter establishing the two agencies. The boards of each agency were merged, and drawn more fully under the oversight of the financial ministries of the governments, and BECC's international advisory council was eliminated. This diminished NGO participation in board decisions and restricted public participation in shaping the new board's agenda. While these measures were taken to streamline the Commission's decision making, enhancing administrative efficiency, in the minds of many environmentalists they were a step back from the promise of the 1993 agreement.[48]

44. Mark Spalding, "Governance Issues under the Environmental Side Agreement to the NAFTA", in Mark J. Spalding (ed.), *Sustainable Development in San Diego-Tijuana* (San Diego, CA: Center for US–Mexican Studies, University of California, San Diego, 1999), p. 68.

45. Border Environment Cooperation Commission (BECC), *2011 Annual Report, Border Environment Cooperation Commission* (Cd. Juarez, Chihuahua: BECC, 2011), p. 6, available: <http://www.becc.org/capacity-building/publications-reports/2011—becc-annual-report>.

46. Debra J. Little, "Transboundary Cooperation in the US–Mexico Border Region", in Cesar M. Fuentes Flores and Sergio Pena Medina (eds.), *Planeacion Binacional y Cooperacion Transfronteriza entre Mexico y Estados Unidos* (Tijuana, Baja California: Colegio de la Frontera Norte, 2005), pp. 64–65.

47. Andrea Abel, "BECC, NADB Stretch to Help Border Communities", Americas Program at the Interhemispheric Resources Center, 4 October 2002, available: <http://www.cipamericas.org/archives/1249>.

48. Paul Ganster, "Letter from Paul Ganster, Chair, GNEB, to the Boards of the BECC and NADB, February 25, 2005", in Good Neighbor Environmental Board, *Air Quality and Transportation and Cultural and*

The North American Development Bank

The BECC's financial partner in project development, the NADB, was from its inception dogged with controversy, in part owing to its greater insularity from the border public and in part a function of the fiscal constraints imposed on its operations by the governments.[49] Under its charter, NADB's lending authority was restricted to loans let at prevailing market rates to prevent it from unfairly competing with private capital. Capitalised at USD 3 billion (85 per cent of which is callable capital, 15 per cent paid-in capital) with USD 405 million available for border environmental programmes, much of this capacity went unutilised early on, reflecting the relative poverty of the border region and its inability to participate in market-level development financing.[50] In 1997 the US Environmental Protection Agency (EPA) stepped in to facilitate project development with a dedicated fund, originally USD 100 million, to be administered by the bank as grants with a small part given over to project development and administered separately by BECC. The two funds, the Border Environmental Infrastructure Fund (BEIF) and the Project Development Assistance Program (PDAP) enabled BECC-NADB to sidestep some of the constraints on the Bank's participation in project financing, strengthening its role as the principal financier of BECC-certified environmental projects along the border.[51] In 2004, the revised BECC-NADB charter allowed NADB to use part of its paid-in capital (profits on its lending) as dedicated grants, supplementing the grants from the EPA.

NADB's accomplishments are closely tied to BECC's as it is largely restricted to financing BECC-certified projects. As originally conceived, the Bank was to be something of a junior partner to BECC at the policy level, limited to a financial supporting role in project design and approval. Since the BECC-NADB board merger in 2004, knowledgeable observers believe the Bank has now assumed the leading role.[52] Nevertheless, the NADB's resources have been central to the infusion of funds in environmental projects along the border. With jurisdictional expansion after 2002, the governments have been able to use NADB to fund a wider range of projects. In August 2002, they supported the creation of a new NADB fund, the Water Conservation Investment Fund, which was instrumental in resolving a contentious international water dispute on the Rio Grande River.[53] More recently, in 2011, NADB launched a new Community Assistance Program (CAP) that extends grants of up to USD 500,000 to support projects across all environmental sectors, with priority given to water and wastewater projects.[54] Unlike BEIF,

Natural Resources (Washington, DC: US Environmental Protection Agency, EPA 130-R-06-002, 2006), p. 49.

49. Robert G. Varady, David Colnic, Robert Merideth and Terry Sprouse, "The US–Mexican Border Environment Commission: Collected Perspectives on the First Two Years", *Journal of Borderlands Studies*, Vol. 11, No. 2 (1996), pp. 89–119.

50. North American Development Bank, *Annual Report 2011, North American Development Bank* (San Antonio, TX, 2011), p. 20.

51. *Ibid.*

52. Spalding, "Addressing Border Environmental Problems", *op. cit.*, p. 125.

53. International Boundary and Water Commission, *Minute 308. United States Allocation of Rio Grande Waters during the Last Year of the Current Cycle* (Cd. Juarez, Chihuahua, 28 June 2002); North American Development Bank, *Annual Report, 2007, North American Development Bank* (San Antonio, TX, 2007), p. 5.

54. North American Development Bank, *Annual Report 2011, op. cit.*, p. 5.

whose funds enable communities to leverage additional funds from NADB and other lenders for BECC-certified projects, the CAP fully funds smaller projects.

The NADB's funds, supplemented by EPA, Mexican agencies and other governmental and private sector sources, are certainly at the heart of the environmental protection initiatives issuing from NAFTA. NADB's ability to grow and plough its own earnings into border environmental infrastructure has gained in recent years, just as EPA's contribution has shrunk, buffering the impact of fiscal austerity on the border area. It can be argued, however, that as beneficial as the BECC-NADB investments have been along the border, their operations have been constrained by lacklustre government support. Evidence of this was particularly visible in 2006, during the administrations of George W. Bush and Vicente Fox, when their respective treasury departments sought, unsuccessfully, to scuttle the NADB, which would in turn have significantly weakened BECC's operations.[55]

The La Paz Agreement Programmes

The project development work of BECC and NADB is fitted diplomatically into the larger framework agreement on border environmental cooperation, the 1983 La Paz Agreement, and is meant to implement and strengthen the work of environmental cooperation along the US–Mexican border. The La Paz Agreement, which grew out of the governments' structural deficiencies in addressing transboundary and border area environmental problems in the 1970s and early 1980s, is an executive agreement intended to strengthen environmental cooperation along the border. It committed the two nations' environmental agencies to meet annually for the purpose of addressing common environmental concerns along the boundary.[56] As a framework agreement, it embraced the full gamut of environmental and natural resources issues but neither set any priorities nor committed funds. However, it did recognise the voices of sub-national governments and non-governmental stakeholders, legitimising broad public participation in the development of any subsidiary agreements and programmes directed to environmental cooperation. It also provided for further agreement as annexes to the La Paz accord.[57]

In the 1980s and during the run-up to NAFTA, the La Paz Agreement was roundly criticised by environmentalists who, despite the realisation of subsidiary agreements on hazardous substances, water and air pollution, faulted its implementation as low priority, poorly funded, ad hoc and falling well short of addressing the mounting environmental pressures in the border region.[58] Thus, an important thrust of the NAFTA-based environmental reforms was to invigorate the La Paz Agreement by initiating what became a series of short- to medium-term implementation agreements between the two countries. These successive programmes under the helm of the two national environmental ministries built on the work of other agencies, particularly BECC-NADB, as part of their operational mission.

55. Ganster, "Letter from Paul Ganster", *op. cit.*, p. 49.

56. *Agreement between the United States of America and the United Mexican States on Cooperation for the Protection and Improvement of the Environment in the Border Area, op. cit.*

57. *Ibid.*, Art. XIV.

58. Stephen P. Mumme, "New Directions in Transboundary Environmental Management: A Critique of Current Proposals", *Natural Resources Journal*, Vol. 32, No. 3 (1992), pp. 539–562.

The first of these programmes, the aforementioned IBEP (1992–1994), was little more than a cobbling together and reframing of the existing measures in place between the two countries, including the sanitation work of the International Boundary and Water Commission (IBWC) and that of the La Paz Agreement environmental working groups established after 1983. Influenced by the United Nations Rio Summit on the Human Environment in 1992, the IBEP also reframed the border environmental programme as guided by the principle of sustainable development. This theme and the workgroup approach were subsequently incorporated into the Border XXI programme (1995–2000), which built on the new functions and financing of BECC and NADB in the area of water and sanitation and expanded the number of binational environmental workgroups to nine. During this period of time, the advent of BECC-NADB investment in water projects drove unprecedented inter-sectoral integration between EPA and IBWC, as seen in the development and funding of an international wastewater treatment plant at San Diego and Tijuana.[59] Systematic assessment of border environmental indicators was initiated and greater effort expended on enforcing environmental regulations.[60] In NAFTA's wake, greater federal funding was provided for a range of border environmental projects. While federal financing supported most of these, US states were encouraged to commit to the projects and some, like Texas, did. Other states and tribal governments resisted participation in the new programmes,[61] arguing that they had been excluded from their design and planning, violating the spirit and promise of the La Paz Agreement.

By 2000, the Border XXI programme could claim a number of important achievements. Environmental infrastructure projects backed by BECC-NADB increased potable water service in Mexican border cities from 88 to 93 per cent coverage between 1995 and 2000.[62] The percentage of Mexican citizens served by wastewater treatment was even more dramatic, jumping from 34 per cent in 1995 to 75 per cent in 2000.[63] Air quality assessment programmes had been set in place in seven urban areas, with abatement programmes in El Paso–Cd. Juarez and Mexicali–Imperial Valley.[64] Six of twelve pairs of sister cities on the border had contingency plans for handling chemical emergencies by 2000, up from zero in 1995.[65] A pilot programme to track hazardous waste trade between the two countries was put in place and helpful diagnostic and interpretative tools developed to facilitate binational tracking and regulation of hazardous wastes.[66] Numerous training workshops were conducted on cooperative environmental enforcement, environmental health, pollution prevention and toxic and hazardous substance management.[67] A serious effort to promote public environmental education

59. International Boundary and Water Commission, *Minute 283. Conceptual Plan for the Solution to the Border Sanitation Problem in San Diego, California/Tijuana, Baja California* (El Paso, TX, 2 July 1990).

60. Environmental Protection Agency, *United States–Mexico Border Environmental Indicators, 1997* (Washington, DC: EPA 909-R-98-001, 1998).

61. Good Neighbor Environmental Board, *Annual Report of the Good Neighbor Environmental Board* (Washington, DC: EPA, GNEB, July 1998), p. 13.

62. Environmental Protection Agency, *US–Mexican Border XXI Program: Progress Report, 1996-2000* (Washington, DC: EPA 160/R/00/001, 2000), p. 131 (on file with author).

63. *Ibid.*, p. 131.

64. *Ibid.*, pp. 27–28.

65. *Ibid.*, p. 57.

66. *Ibid.*, pp. 90–91.

67. *Ibid.*, pp. 54, 63, 71, 117.

complemented these various achievements.[68] Three border area public information and outreach offices were established in the border region's major urban areas.[69] Addressing jurisdictional issues and stakeholder criticism, the EPA in coordination with Mexico's Secretariat of Environment, Natural Resources, and Fisheries (SEMARNAP) also reached better understandings with states and tribal governments concerning their participation in the La Paz programmes.[70]

The election of more conservative governments in both countries in 2000, however, ushered in retrenchment. A new 10-year border programme, Border 2012, unveiled in September 2002, revamped border environmental management in a decentralised direction, with corresponding reductions in federal support.[71] The nine binational border-wide workgroups model was jettisoned in favour of a system of border-wide policy forums on air, water and toxic pollution, a more limited number of border-wide workgroups dealing with environmental health, emergency response and cooperative enforcement, four regional workgroups, and local, issue-specific task forces strategically focused on five overarching goals: reducing water contamination, reducing air pollution, reducing land contamination, reducing exposure to pesticides, and improving chemical safety.[72] Administrative tensions in the US between EPA and the Interior Department led to natural resource concerns being dropped from the border programme.

In principle, the decentralising thrust of the new border programme had its virtues and might have been effective in building the partnerships and mobilising public support behind border area environmental cooperation.[73] But given the relative poverty and resource limitations of the border area, federal support was still needed on both sides of the border. Instead, EPA and SEMARNAT financing steadily fell, best exemplified in a 90 per cent drop in BEIF grant funding at NADB by 2007 but also felt directly in cutbacks to task force support.[74] A highly critical mid-term review of Border 2012 by EPA auditors in 2007, which prompted a revision of the programme's aims, strategies, and procedures in 2008, may also have inadvertently further diminished US support for the programme.[75] Restrictive national security policies in the United States and a rise in narco-violence in the latter

68. *Ibid.*, pp. 79–86.

69. *Ibid.*, p. 12.

70. *Ibid.*, Appendix XI.

71. Environmental Protection Agency, *Border 2012: US–Mexico Environmental Program* (Washington, DC: EPA-160-R-03-001, 2003).

72. *Ibid.*, p. 21. In 2003, goals four and five were amended and stretched into a new goal four (improve environmental health), goal five (enhance joint readiness for environmental response) and goal six (improve environmental performance). Two border-wide task forces were also established: a Border-wide Communications Task Force and a Border-wide Indicators Task Force. See Environmental Protection Agency, *US–Mexico Environmental Program: Border 2012, a Mid-Course Refinement (2008–2012)* (Washington, DC: EPA-909-R-08-003, 2008).

73. Hecht et al., *op. cit.*

74. Good Neighbor Environmental Board, *Natural Disasters and the Environment along the US–Mexico Border* (Washington, DC: EPA-130-R-08-002, 2008), pp. 51–53. EPA's budget for border environmental affairs is difficult to track as, with the exception of BEIF, appropriations are buried in the budgets of other EPA programmes at the Region 6 and Region 9 offices who then sub-allocate resources to border affairs. See GAO, *op. cit.* The fact that EPA has never had a direct line item budget for the border environmental programme speaks to its relatively low priority at the agency.

75. Environmental Protection Agency, *Evaluation Report: Border 2012 Program Needs to Improve Program Management to Ensure Results* (Washington, DC: EPA, Office of the Inspector General, Report No. 08-P-0245, September 2008), available: <http://www.epa.gov/oig/reports/2008/20080903-08-P-0245.pdf>.

part of the decade further stressed cross-border cooperation, stalling progress and, in the case of some task forces, practically eliminating non-governmental public participation.[76]

At its close in 2012, the Border 2012 programme could still claim a number of valuable accomplishments. Water-related projects under the Border Water Infrastructure Program and backed by BECC-NADB again topped the list, with 92 certified water projects by 2010, and investment of USD 1.7 billion in water projects. Between 2006 and 2010, 44 water projects were completed, and 35 of these provided first-time service to border residents, extending service to 53 per cent of the 98,575 homes found lacking in services in 2003.[77] Overall, the number of environmental infrastructure projects reached 167, with USD 3.6 billion invested.[78] For air quality, some gains had been made in extending air quality monitoring, although of five established monitoring areas along the border only at El Paso and Cd. Juarez was air quality monitored binationally.[79] The lack of comparable cross-border data continued to plague consistent air quality assessment along the border. A new border programme for retrofitting diesel-powered trucks and buses with emissions controls was adopted with Border 2012 support and a programme of identifying greenhouse gas emitters begun.[80] A solid waste programme introduced in 2004 aimed at reducing the many discarded tyre dumps in Mexico had eliminated 6.9 million tyres by 2009, with a 300 per cent increase in annual tyre recovery by 2012.[81] By 2008 the two countries had also cleaned up one of the most notorious hazardous waste sites along the border, the Metales y Derivados lead smelter site in Tijuana, the subject of the CEC investigation mentioned earlier.[82]

In sum, the La Paz Agreement border programmes have raised the profile of border area environmental problems since NAFTA entered into effect. Even subtracting the water and sanitation project work completed under the Border Water Infrastructure Program, the Border XXI and Border 2012 programmes have been valuable in addressing critical border environmental issues and sustaining a binational dialogue on environmental protection among governmental and non-governmental entities in the border region. Yet it is also clear that national support for these programmes, including the water and sanitation programmes, has waned significantly since the mid-1990s, a fact not lost on the GNEB.[83] The

76. Allyson Siwik, Elaine Hebard and Celso Jacques, "A Critical Review of Public Participation in Environmental Decision Making along the US–Mexican Border. Lessons from Border 2012 and Suggestions for Future Programs", in Erik Lee and Paul Ganster (eds.), *The US–Mexican Border Environment: Progress and Challenges for Sustainability* (San Diego, CA: Southwest Center for Environmental Research and Policy, Monograph Series No. l, San Diego State University Press, 2012), pp. 105–144.

77. Environmental Protection Agency, *Border 2012: US–Mexico Environmental Program. State of the Border Region Indicators Report, 2010* (Washington, DC: EPA, May 2011), pp. 25–26, available: <http://www2.epa.gov/sites/production/files/documents/border-2012_indicator-rpt_eng.pdf>.

78. *Ibid.*, pp. 23–25.

79. *Ibid.*, p. 54.

80. *Ibid.*, p. 58.

81. *Ibid.*, p. 71.

82. Environmental Health Coalition (EHC), *What We Do. Border Environmental Justice: Metales y Derivados Toxic Site* (San Diego, CA: EHC, 2011), available: <http://www.environmentalhealth.org/index.php/en/what-we-do/border-environmental-justice/metales-y-derivados-toxic-site>.

83. Good Neighbor Environmental Board, *Environmental, Economic, and Health Status of Water Resources along the US–Mexico Board, Fifteenth Report of the Good Neighbor Environmental Board to the President of the United States* (Washington, DC: EPA and GNEB, EPA-130-R-12-001, 2012), p. 9.

newest iteration of the border programmes, dubbed Border 2020, largely based on Border 2012, must reckon with these fiscal and political constraints.[84]

The Challenge of Public Involvement

As seen in the preceding discussion, the NAFTA agreement mobilised environmental concern in an unprecedented manner both with respect to the trade agreement writ large and the border environment in particular. Environmentalists hoped the NAFTA-related institutional reforms would create new venues for public participation and citizen engagement with border environmental protection. They were not altogether disappointed, but nearly 20 years later it is evident that environmental mobilisation and public participation have not been steadily ascendant, are fragmented and have suffered setbacks.

Advancing public participation in border environmental protection was incorporated as an objective of the La Paz programmes, beginning with the IBEP in 1992.[85] It was also a goal of the BECC and NADB and, in a more broadly gauged fashion, incorporated as a core objective of the CEC. As documented by Daniel Sabet with specific reference to border water policy, the NAFTA reforms created new political opportunities for civil society organisations to pursue environmental improvements in the border region.[86] At least a dozen new cross-border environmental advocacy partnerships and coalitions were established during and after the NAFTA reforms with interest in the border water sector.[87] New advocacy groups were created and old ones were energised. Under the umbrella of the La Paz Process, national advisory bodies were created in both countries and Border XXI working groups collaborated with NGOs. Environmental information centres were established, as noted previously. Border 2012's decentralised task forces provided further opportunities for public participation, joining governments and citizen-based groups in environmental problem solving. BECC's original board and advisory structure represented civil society and NGOs as well as governmental stakeholders.[88] Its project certification process required citizen advisory boards as part of its commitment to sustainable development. At CEC, the Article 14 citizen submission process, project advisory boards and an advocacy group grant programme, the North American Fund for Environmental Cooperation (NAFEC), all promoted public engagement in work related to the border environment. By 1999, even the historically insular IBWC had begun to open doors, establishing new citizen committees and embracing the concept of sustainable development of the water resources under its jurisdiction.[89]

Taken as a set, these various reforms helped to legitimise, institutionalise and broaden public participation in border area environmental affairs and in this

84. Environmental Protection Agency, *Border 2020: US–Mexico Environmental Program* (Washington, DC: EPA-60-R-12-001, 2012), available: <http://www.epa.gov/region9/border/pdf/border2020summary.pdf>.

85. Environmental Protection Agency, *Integrated Environmental Plan for the Mexican–US Border Area, 1992–1994* (Washington, DC: EPA, A92-171.toc, 1992), p. V-48; Gregory, *op. cit.*, p. 172.

86. Daniel Sabet, *Nonprofits and their Networks* (Tucson, AZ: University of Arizona Press, 2007).

87. *Ibid.*, p. 140.

88. "Agreement Concerning the Establishment of a Border Environment Cooperation Commission and a North American Development Bank", 1993; *op. cit.*; Siwik et al., *op. cit.*

89. International Boundary and Water Commission, United States Section (USIBWC), *Strategic Plan* (El Paso, TX: USIBWC, 3 December 2000).

sense may be considered net gains for environmental activism.[90] Compared to the state of affairs in 1990, the border today has more participatory opportunities in the environmental arena.

However, some of these gains have eroded since 2000.[91] In brief, reduced funding of Border 2012 task forces is an obstacle to binational participation, particularly for those on the Mexican side of the border.[92] Further complications arise from US border security operations that add to the time and expense of cross-border commuting and are often attended by forms of security-related intimidation that discourage cross-border commuting.[93] At BECC, the 2004 changes to BECC and NADB's mandate that eliminated the binational advisory board reduced the opportunity for independent advocacy groups to be closely involved with BECC-NADB policy. At the project level, as nicely documented by Jo Marie Rios and Joseph Jozwiak for the Texas–Mexico border,[94] BECC's management of citizen advisory boards for particular projects has limited the opportunity for environmental advocacy groups to influence project development and certification. At CEC, abandonment of NAFEC in 2002 eliminated a small but important source of seed funding for border region environmental groups.[95] The reduction of philanthropic support for border environmental groups at funders like the Ford Foundation has also hindered border area environmental advocacy. An example of this is the abandonment of the Ford Foundation-sponsored annual Binational Environmental Forum (Encuentro Binacional Ambiental), which had brought border area environmentalists together for networking and discussion for five years, running between 1997 and 2002, and facilitated binational coalition building.[96] While many of the transboundary environmental coalitions listed by Sabet are still active, at least one has ceased and others have seen declining membership.[97] In general, NGO participation in Border 2012 diminished as the programme neared an end, presenting an immediate challenge for its successor, the Border 2020 programme. Perhaps reflecting this reality, the new programme's guiding principles seek to improve "stakeholder

90. Mario Alberto Velasquez Garcia, "Perspectivas del movimiento ambiental en la frontera entre Mexico y Estados Unidos. Acciones y necesidades", *Region y Sociedad,* Vol. 19, num. especial (2007), p. 189.

91. Stephen P. Mumme, "Reflections on Public Participation in Environmental Protection Policy on the US–Mexico Border", in Departamento de Estudios Urbanos y Medio Ambiente (coordinador), *Retos ambientales y desarrollo urbano en la frontera Mexico-Estados Unidos* (Tijuana: Colegio de la Frontera Norte, 2009), pp. 227–252.

92. For a US example, see Siwik et al., *op. cit.*, p. 122.

93. Paul Ganster, "Environmental Protection and US–Mexican Border Security: The Border Fence in Context", in Carlos A. de La Parra and Ana Cordova (eds.), *A Barrier to our Shared Environment: The Border Fence between the United States and Mexico* (Mexico, D.F.: Secretariat of Environment and Natural Resources, 2007), pp. 34–35.

94. Jo Marie Rios and Joseph Jozwiak, "NAFTA and the Border Environmental Cooperation Commission: Assessing Activism in the Environmental Infrastructure Project Certification Process (1996–2004)", *Journal of Borderlands Studies,* Vol. 23, No. 2 (2008), pp. 76–78.

95. Mumme and Lybecker, *op. cit.*

96. Diana M. Liverman, Robert G. Varady, Octavio Chavez and Roberto Sanchez, "Environmental Issues along the United States Border: Drivers of Change and Responses of Citizens and Institutions", *Annual Review of Energy and Environment,* Vol. 24 (1999), p. 629.

97. The Rio Grande/Rio Bravo Coalition, for example, practically folded in the mid-2000s, but has recently been resuscitated in a more limited form. The Tijuana River Watershed Border Visioning Project produced a report in 2005 and is no longer active.

participation and ensure broad-based representation from the environmental, public health, and other relevant sectors."[98]

Managing Trade's Threat to the Border Environment: A Reform Agenda

Just six years after NAFTA entered into force, World Watch analyst Hillary French would argue with reference to the US–Mexican border that "[d]espite the environmental side agreement that accompanied NAFTA, conditions have improved little and may even have deteriorated in the years since, as more US companies have flocked to the region."[99] Many environmentalists shared her scepticism. Even if NAFTA had not triggered a regulatory "race to the bottom" in the environmental arena, as a Carnegie report noted in 2004,[100] it plainly stimulated greater border industrialisation and urbanisation, amplifying stressors on the border environment. From just under 1,500 *maquiladoras* located on the border in 1990, their number rose to 2,300 plants by 2005.[101] Between 1990 and 2005, Mexico's border state population grew from 13.2 million inhabitants to 18.2 million, an increase of 37 per cent in just 15 years, with much of this increase located in border cities.[102] Truck traffic rose dramatically at ports of entry as the value of land-based freight movement, for example, rose 150 per cent between 1995 and 2009.[103]

Have the NAFTA-based environmental reforms mitigated the adverse environmental consequences of such trade-induced growth? Partly. There can be little doubt, for example, that the water and wastewater infrastructure coverage along the US–Mexico border is better than it was in 1993. This is no mean achievement, and reflects the considerable investment made along the border through BECC and NADB with the support of the EPA's Border Water Infrastructure Program and the facilities of BEIF and PDAP. Paved roads help to mitigate the air quality impact of rapid urbanisation, as do investments in sanitary landfills and programmes that improve the efficiency of brick-making kilns. Community-based environmental education initiatives help to reduce exposures to lead-based paint and other toxic products. In general, the level of local, state, tribal and federal awareness of environmental problems and the opportunity to cooperate across the border in addressing these issues is greater than it was in 1994.

The problem, of course, is that trade's impact on border development continually outstrips governance capacity to deal with its adverse environmental effects. In the area of water and wastewater infrastructure provision, urban expansion continues to race ahead of service provision, leading the GNEB to affirm that the border's prevailing water infrastructure needs far exceed what the governments have been willing to spend.[104] Two decades after NAFTA, the Mexican border region still lacks adequate hazardous waste disposal facilities despite the surge in *maquiladora*

98. EPA, *Border 2020: US–Mexico Environmental Program*, *op. cit.*, p. 1.

99. Hillary French, *Vanishing Borders* (Washington, DC: World Watch Institute, 2000), p. 84.

100. Audley, "Introduction", *op. cit.*, p. 7.

101. Anderson and Gerber, *op. cit.*, p. 91.

102. Paul Ganster and David E. Lorey, The U.S. –Mexican Border into the Twenty-First Century, 2nd edn (New York: Rowman & Littlefield, 2008), p. 17.

103. EPA, *Border 2012: US–Mexico Environmental Program. State of the Border Region Indicators Report, 2010*, *op. cit.*, p. 12.

104. Good Neighbor Environmental Board, *Environmental, Economic, and Health Status of Water Resources*, *op. cit.*, pp. 7–9, 48.

development. The absence until recently of well-designed environmental indicator assessment limits the ability to gauge environmental progress, contributing to the Border 2012 programme's reputation as a series of ad hoc programmes with modest impact on the border region.

More than a decade ago, the GNEB in its evaluation of progress of the Border XXI programme observed that "a precise reading of the (Border XXI) Framework Document clarifies that the Program's goal is to promote sustainable development without having a parallel aspiration to achieve it."[105] This is still true, even as the Border 2020 programme takes effect. Both project development through BECC and NADB and the recent La Paz programme still have the look of a collection of programmes less driven by strategic commitment to the sustainable development of the border region and more the result of ad hoc accommodation to the variable and generally declining commitments of the governments.[106] Despite occasional high-profile initiatives,[107] bilateral cooperation on natural resource management has been disconnected from the La Paz Process for more than a decade and has severely suffered from the imposition of security measures that are highly disruptive of ecosystems in the border area.[108]

The unilateral border security programmes implemented by the United States are themselves one of the unanticipated consequences of intensified bilateral trade. Border analyst Peter Andreas has convincingly argued that US security measures are directly tied to trade expansion which, on the one hand, undermines rural production in Mexico (the basis of much Mexican migration to the US) and, on the other, accentuates fear of integrating processes in North America for which heightened border security is a convenient policy sop.[109] Add to this picture the diminution of federal funding of binational environmental initiatives and declining public participation in environmental programmes, and it is clear that the environmental protection and sustainable development commitments now in place have not kept pace with the border's globalising trends. They have certainly not advanced a coherent agenda of ecological modernisation in the region.

What does such a strategic agenda of ecological modernisation along the border entail? Most importantly, it means revitalised support for public participation, voice and information access bearing on border environmental programmes. This should include new binational venues and generous subsidies for public engagement meant to bridge the asymmetries that so often impede binational collaboration in border affairs. It certainly requires an integrated, multisectoral approach to environmental protection and sustainable development tied to

---

105. EPA, *US–Mexican Border XXI Program: Progress Report, 1996–2000, op. cit.*, Addendum No. 1, p. 9.

106. Roberto Sánchez-Rodríguez and Stephen P. Mumme, "Environmental Protection and Natural Resources", in Peter Smith and Andrew Seeley (eds.), *Mexico and the United States: The Politics of Partnership* (Boulder, CO: Lynne-Rienner Press, 2013), pp. 139–159.

107. White House, "Joint Statement from President Barack Obama and President Felipe Calderon" (Washington, DC: White House, Office of the Press Secretary, 19 May 2010), available: <http://www.whitehouse.gov/the-press-office/joint-statement-president-barack-obama-and-president-felipe-calder-n>.

108. Carlos de la Parra and Ana Cordova, "The Border Fence and the Assault on Principles", in de La Parra and Cordova, *A Barrier to our Shared Environment, op. cit.*, pp. 175–183; Eduardo Riemann, "Ecological Risks Involved in the Construction of the Border Fence", in de La Parra and Cordova, *A Barrier to our Shared Environment, op. cit.*, pp. 105–114; Rurik List, "The Impacts of the Border Fence on Wild Mammals", in de La Parra and Cordova, *A Barrier to our Shared Environment, op. cit.*, pp. 77–86.

109. Peter Andreas, *Border Games: Policing the US–Mexico Divide*, 2nd edn (Ithaca, NY: Cornell University Press, 2009), pp. 105, 141–145.

targeted and timed improvements in environmental conditions and quality of life measures in the border region. It means incorporating climate change into national and binational planning horizons. It requires calibration of water, mining, energy, transportation and other urban and agricultural development with the attainment of quality of life objectives along the border—starting with the adoption of the long-proposed US–Mexico or US–Canada–Mexico agreement on transboundary environmental assessment. It requires strengthened enforcement of environmental regulations and more rigorous oversight of industrial activities on both sides of the border. It requires reforming binational diplomatic procedures to facilitate the transboundary movement and cooperation of resource specialists and environmental managers along the border. It means harnessing national security concerns to environmental protection and environmental security and strengthening and reimagining the operations of binational and trinational agencies with environmental remits. It certainly means reversing the trend towards declining funding for environmental assessment, planning and regulation along the border. At the systemic level it requires investing in Mexican development and adjusting the economic playing field across the border, something NAFTA has failed to do.

In sum, if the more apocalyptic environmental scenarios attached to NAFTA have not materialised, it is evident that the dynamics of rapid industrialisation, urbanisation and amplified cross-border trade continue to outstrip environmental improvements and binational cooperative initiatives in the border area. In this respect, the US–Mexican border offers important lessons for students of globalisation. It shows that the international commitments to trade liberalisation are likely to exceed the international and intergovernmental commitments to environmental mitigation irrespective of the rhetoric associated with those agreements. It points to the political vulnerability of international commitments to environmental protection over time. It calls into question the effectiveness of international environmental accords unsupported by firm, long-term financial commitments for their realisation. It demonstrates why a strategic vision for the sustainable development of the border region is vital in confronting globalising trends. And it suggests that some of the rhetoric of sustainable development, particularly those arguments advancing decentralised, subsidiary solutions to the environmental challenges presented by free trade, may be inadequate for addressing the effects of globalisation where substantial socio-economic and political asymmetries prevail, as they do along this border. Strong national commitments are needed to confront the environmental externalities that come with liberalised trade and we can only hope that a reinvigoration of national investment in environmental protection will be forthcoming along the US–Mexican border.

One Bioregion/One Health: An Integrative Narrative for Transboundary Planning along the US–Mexico Border

KEITH PEZZOLI, JUSTINE KOZO, KAREN FERRAN,
WILMA WOOTEN, GUDELIA RANGEL GOMEZ and
WAEL K. AL-DELAIMY

Global megatrends—including climate change, food and water insecurity, economic crisis, large-scale disasters and widespread increases in preventable diseases—are motivating a bioregionalisation of planning in city-regions around the world. Bioregionalisation is an emergent process. It is visible where societies have begun grappling with complex socio-ecological problems by establishing place-based (territorial) approaches to securing health and well-being. This article examines a bioregional effort to merge place-based health planning and ecological restoration along the US–Mexico border. The theoretical construct underpinning this effort is called One Bioregion/One Health (OBROH). OBROH frames health as a transborder phenomenon that involves human–animal–environment interactions. The OBROH approach aims to improve transborder knowledge networking, ecosystem resilience, community participation in science–society relations, leadership development and cross-disciplinary training. It is a theoretically informed narrative to guide action. OBROH is part of a paradigm shift evident worldwide; it is redefining human–ecological relationships in the quest for healthy place making. The article concludes on a forward-looking note about the promise of environmental epidemiology, telecoupling, ecological restoration, the engaged university and bioregional justice as concepts pertinent to reinventing place-based planning.

Introduction

The 21st century's socio-economic, ecological and environmental public health problems are increasingly complex and globally interwoven.[1] Our capacity to address these problems (e.g. climate change, food and water insecurity, economic crisis, large-scale disasters and widespread increases in preventable diseases) hinges on our ability to foster authentic and equitable collaboration among diverse, sometimes conflicting, interests. Narratives are key to framing collaborative efforts.[2] This article sketches a narrative called One Bioregion/One Health (OBROH). The

1. Bill McKibben, *Earth: Making a Life on a Tough New Planet* (New York: Time Books, 2010); F. Biermann, K. Abbott, S. Andresen, K. Bäckstrand et al., "Navigating the Anthropocene: Improving Earth System Governance", *Science*, Vol. 335, No. 6074 (2012), pp. 1306–1307.

2. Semour J. Mandlebaum, "Narrative and Other Tools", in Barbara J. Eckstein and James A. Throgmorton (eds.), *Story and Sustainability: Planning, Practice, and Possibility for American Cities* (Cambridge, MA: MIT Press, 2003), ch. 8.

OBROH narrative interweaves (1) emergent discourse in urban and regional planning that focuses on the built environment in relationship to health (e.g. urban design for walkability and active living, watershed management for pollution prevention) with (2) emergent discourse in public health and epidemiology that widens the circle of concern for human health to include human–animal–environment interactions. These two discourses have begun to document how ecosystem integrity is vital to human as well as non-human health. In this light, ecological restoration is becoming an important part of the health equation. Utilising the US–Mexico border as a case in point, this article cites examples of how OBROH has been embraced to promote environmental health, security and justice. The focus is on initiatives aimed at improving health outcomes on both sides of the border by improving transboundary institutional networking, risk assessment, monitoring, communication and ecological restoration.

Ecological restoration "is the process of assisting the recovery of an ecosystem that has been degraded, damaged, or destroyed."[3] Restoration is typically applied as an act of renewal, revival or reinvigoration to enhance the ability of ecosystems to change as their environments change. Ecological restoration is driven by a range of organisations with diverse interests, including wilderness managers striving for high levels of ecological integrity; ranchers needing sustainable soils; and residents of sister cities such as San Diego in the United States and Tijuana in Mexico who want clean, reliable water supplies and a healthy environment. Urban ecological restoration is a critical need for US–Mexico border residents because border communities face heightened environmental and public health risks associated with ecosystem degradation (e.g. risks arising from floods, fire, dust, water contamination and newly emergent disease vectors).[4] Ecological restoration in urban areas, as part of a broader bioregional/watershed approach as articulated by OBROH, can increase the positive impacts of restored soils, air and watersheds, as well as provide many important socio-economic and health benefits.

The US–Mexico Border Region

There are many places worldwide where urban growth contiguously spans an international border. These "transfrontier metropolises"[5] often have health risks in common on both sides of the border. The US–Mexico border region—defined as a swath of land 100 kilometres north and 100 kilometres south of the entire international boundary—has an estimated 15 million people mostly concentrated in 14 binational sister cities. The border extends 3,168 kilometres with 52 legal land crossing points (a place where a vehicle can travel by road or rail from US to Mexican territory).[6] It is one of the busiest international land frontiers in the world.

3. Society for Ecological Restoration, "SER International Primer on Ecological Restoration", cited 18 June 2014, available: <http://www.ser.org/resources/resources-detail-view/ser-international-primer-on-ecological-restoration> (accessed 18 June 2014).

4. US Environmental Protection Agency, Border 2012: US–Mexico Environmental Program, "State of the Border Region Indicators Report", available: <http://www2.epa.gov/border2020/indicators-report> (accessed 18 June 2014).

5. Lawrence A. Herzog, "Cross-National Urban Structure in the Era of Global Cities: The US–Mexico Transfrontier Metropolis", *Urban Studies*, Vol. 28 (1991), pp. 519–533.

6. Research Institute, Western Washington University, "Atlas of the Land Entry Ports on the US–Mexico Border", Border Policy Brief, 2010, available: <http://www.wwu.edu/bpri/files/2010_Fall_Border_Brief.pdf> (accessed 26 June 2014).

The Good Neighbor Environmental Board (GNEB), an appointed independent US federal advisory committee, has been addressing environmental issues along the US–Mexico border for over 15 years.[7] The GNEB's mission is to advise the US president and Congress on good neighbour practices and issue an annual report with recommendations focused on environmental infrastructure needs within the US states contiguous to Mexico. The 16th annual GNEB report—scheduled for publication in late 2014—will focus on ecological restoration. GNEB members determine the specific content of the annual reports in a deliberative process open to the public. One recommendation under consideration for the 2014 report is a call to support ecological restoration in transborder metropolitan areas where urban sprawl is taking place, such as the canyon lands of Tijuana and the river valley of Ciudad Juarez. Recommendations of this sort suggest ways to cross-pollinate the twin objectives of transboundary environmental management and healthy city-region planning.

The health of the Tijuana River Estuary, to cite one illustration, hinges on what happens upstream in the binational Tijuana River Watershed (TRW), a large 4,465 square kilometre watershed two-thirds of which lies in Mexico and one-third in the US. The estuary drains the TRW. Sediment, waste tyres, raw sewage, contaminated storm water and invasive species all flow into the estuary from the rapidly urbanising watershed. These inputs have been recognised, and management with a watershed approach (i.e., place-based strategies that take into account biogeography and water flow paths) is currently getting much attention at the Tijuana River. Two notable collaborative efforts include the Tijuana River Valley Recovery Team and the International Boundary and Water Commissions Watershed Initiative effort for the Tijuana River Valley. Using the watershed as the unit of analysis and framework for intervention is important when addressing ecological restoration and environmental public health. The Tijuana River Valley is home to a variety of birds and other wildlife but it is not only biodiversity that is at risk. Human health is also potentially at risk. The estuary is a filter but it is an overloaded filter and the health of the communities surrounding the estuary depends on the health of the estuary. The estuary is also home to antibiotic-resistant bacteria and mosquitoes that could carry West Nile, dengue and yellow fever.[8] Water contaminated with sewage often flows into the estuary, leading to beach closures north of the river mouth on the US side of the border (notably in Imperial Beach, the Tijuana Slough National Wildlife Refuge, and Border Field State Park).

The contiguously urbanised Mexicali–Calexico transborder metropolis (Mexicali being on the Mexican side, Calexico on the US side) is another of the border region's twin cities. The Mexicali–Calexico twin city is located in a shared valley region known as the Mexicali Valley on the Mexico side and the Imperial Valley on the US side. The New River that runs through this twin city is one of the most polluted in the United States.[9] Its south-to-north flow through the valley from Mexico into the US, ending up in the Salton Sea, drains agricultural and urban runoff containing pesticides, raw sewage, industrial waste and many other contaminants. Although there

7. See GNEB website: <http://www.epa.gov/ocempage/gneb/gneb_president_reports.htm>.

8. Mike Vizzier, Chief of Hazardous Materials Division, Department of Environmental Health, San Diego County, personal communication, 19 March 2014.

9. New River Improvement Project Technical Advisory Committee (TAC), "Strategic Plan: New River Improvement Project", Special Assistant Nilan Watmore (ed.), California Environmental Protection Agency, California–Mexico Border Relations Council, 2011.

are no epidemiological studies to demonstrate it, residents along the path of the New River on the US side attribute clusters of cancer to the toxicants in the waterway.[10] Efforts to scientifically link such cancers to the New River have been hampered by the difficulty of determining the degree of human exposure to the toxicants carried by the river. Cancer develops over decades and a large number of cancer cases with appropriate exposure assessment and lifestyle history are needed to delineate such an association. A large population of Mexican residents in Mexicali is probably exposed to similar contaminants from the New River. A bioregional-scale epidemiological study along the New River on both sides of the border would help shed light on the health risks faced by people living in the shared valley.

The two examples noted above (urban growth in the Tijuana River Valley and along the New River) underscore the potential value of promoting healthy city planning within a bioregional framework.

Healthy City Planning

Healthy city planning addresses how socio-ecological conditions (e.g. environmental quality, poverty, education levels, public safety, human settlement patterns) shape patterns of death and disease including the expression of biologic traits, population distributions of disease, and social inequalities in health. Jason Corburn describes how society and the field of public health have a tendency to search "for one *big cause* or explanation of differences in health outcomes across populations, from nineteenth-century theories of miasma and contagion to medical care and genetic explanations of the twenty-first century."[11] It is now proposed that this issue is far more complicated. The US–Mexico border region is a prime place to integrate healthy city planning and the concept of One Health within a bioregional framework. One Health advocates argue, "larger and more sustainable health benefits will result if research and interventions are collaborative across human, animal (domestic and wildlife), and ecosystem health sectors rather than targeted at each of these factors individually and in isolation from each other."[12]

Urban health researchers and professionals are exploring "how a combination of place-based physical, economic and social characteristics and the public policies and institutions that shape them—not just genetics, lifestyles or health care—are the cause of inequitable distributions of well-being in cities."[13] Public health researchers refer to epigenetics, which suggests that genetic expression (which can give rise to cancer or other diseases) or cellular phenotype (observable physical characteristics or traits) may be caused by mechanisms other than DNA—for instance environmental exposures. Epigenetics is defined as a bridge between genotype (the inherited instructions embodied within an organism's genetic code) and phenotype and is a phenomenon that changes the final outcome of a

10. Perlita R. Dicochea, "Between Borderlands and Bioregionalism: Life-Place Lessons along a Polluted River", *Journal of Borderlands Studies*, Vol. 25 (2010), pp. 19–36.

11. Jason Corburn, *Toward the Healthy City: People, Places, and the Politics of Urban Planning*, Urban and Industrial Environments Series (Cambridge, MA: MIT Press, 2009), p. 3; emphasis added.

12. Patricia A. Conrad, Laura A. Meek and Joe Dumit, "Operationalizing a One Health Approach to Global Health Challenges", *Comparative Immunology, Microbiology and Infectious Diseases*, Vol. 36 (2013), pp. 211–216 (at p. 211).

13. Corburn, *Toward the Healthy City*, *op. cit.*, p. 4.

locus or chromosome without changing the underlying DNA sequence.[14] In other words, our health is not entirely hard wired genetically speaking (i.e., there is some plasticity in gene expression that goes beyond what we inherit from our parents). Public health researchers are beginning to take into account cumulative health risks posed by environmental exposures, stress, diet and behaviour. From this perspective, the qualities of a place (as measured, for instance, by the condition of its air, water, land, safety, neighbourliness, access to fresh fruits and vegetables, built environment and infrastructure for active living like walking and biking) are key determinants of health.[15] Herein lies the theoretical and practical justification for merging the One Bioregion concept with the One Health concept

One Bioregion/One Health

The One Bioregion/One Health (OBROH) narrative frames health as a transborder phenomenon involving human–animal–environment interactions. The OBROH approach aims to improve transborder knowledge networks, ecosystems, green infrastructure, community participation, science–society relations, leadership development, cross-disciplinary training and innovation. It is a theoretically informed narrative to guide action. OBROH is part of a paradigm shift evident worldwide; it is redefining human–ecological relationships in the quest for healthy and resilient place making (see Figure 1).[16]

OBROH reflects a growing understanding that the risks to health are multiple and cumulative. This new approach to healthy urban and regional planning goes beyond identifying individual biology and behaviours as the causal factors determining health disparities and well-being. This new approach emphasises how built environments (e.g. housing, modes of transportation, green infrastructure, spaces for walking, biking and active living) and population health interact—all within the regional biogeography and ecosystems of particular places.

The Bioregionalisation of Health Policy and Planning

Scholars are calling for more place-based ecological integrity along borders where city-regions have in effect become transfrontier societies.[17] The OBROH narrative is one of the responses to this quest to achieve ecological integrity through place-

14. J.M. McGinnis and W.H. Foege, "Actual Causes of Death in the United States", *Journal of the American Medical Association*, Vol. 270, No. 18 (1993), pp. 2207–2212.

15. J.M. McGinnis and Brian W. Powers, "Healthy People and the Design Sciences: The Robert Wood Johnson Foundation Advances the Frontier", *American Journal of Preventive Medicine*, Vol. 43 (2012), pp. 407–409; J.A. Patz et al., "Human Health: Ecosystem Regulation of Infectious Diseases", in R. Scholes and N. Ash (eds.), *Ecosystems and Human Well Being: Current State and Trends: Findings of the Conditions and Trends Working Group by Millennium Ecosystem Assessment* (Washington, DC: Island Press, 2005), pp. 123–142.

16. John Friedmann, "Place and Place-Making in Cities: A Global Perspective", *Planning Theory & Practice*, Vol. 11 (2010), pp. 149–165; Andrew L. Dannenberg, Howard Frumkin and Richard Jackson, *Making Healthy Places: Designing and Building for Health, Well-Being, and Sustainability* (Washington, DC: Island Press, 2011); Jason Corburn, *Healthy City Planning: From Neighbourhood to National Health Equity, Planning, History and Environment Series* (New York: Routledge, 2013).

17. Lawrence A. Herzog, *Shared Space: Rethinking the US–Mexico Border Environment*, US–Mexico Contemporary Perspectives Series (La Jolla, CA: Center for US–Mexican Studies, University of California, San Diego, 2000).

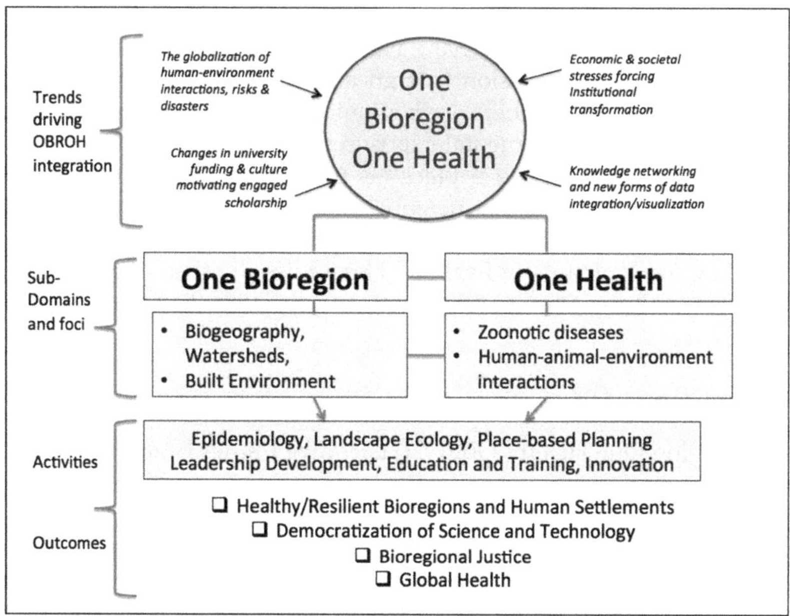

Figure 1. One Bioregion/One Health: Domains, Activities, and Outcomes.

based approaches. At the heart of bioregional theory and practice is this core guiding principle: human beings are social animals; if we are to survive as a species we need healthy relationships and secure attachments with one another *and* with the land, waters, habitat, plants and animals upon which we depend. This is not a new principle; bioregional scholars, ethicists, poets and leaders of bioregional movements around the world have been embracing it for decades.[18]

Bioregion as a term combines the Greek word for life (*bios*) with the Latin word for territory (*regia*) and the Latin term for ruling/governing (*regere*). Bioregion thus means "life territory" or "lifeplace." The bioregionalisation of health policy and planning faces three major challenges: (1) Rebuilding urban and rural communities—on a human scale—to nurture a healthy sense of place, secure attachments and rootedness among community inhabitants; (2) Reintegrating nature and human settlements in ways that holistically instil eco-efficiency, resilience, equity and green cultural values into systems of production, consumption and daily life; and (3) Making known (and valuing) how wildlands, working landscapes, ecological services and rural livelihoods enable cities to exist. To meet these three challenges, bioregionalists advocate localisation. Localisation includes strategies designed to create sustainable and resilient communities on a human scale by fostering local investments in nearby natural resources, rooted livelihoods and

18. The Planet Drum Foundation (www.planetdrum.org) and the Bioregional Congress (www.bioregionalcongress.net) have been documenting and archiving the congresses. An increasing number of universities now offer degrees in bioregionalism, including many in the USA (e.g., University of Idaho; Utah State University; University of California, Davis; Montana State University; and University of Pennsylvania). Bioregional programmes can also be found at universities in Mexico, Asia, Europe and Australia among other places.

institutions thereby augmenting a community's assets (including community power/capabilities).[19]

The spatial scale of bioregional initiatives varies. Bioregionalists focus on watersheds ("ridge top to ridge top"), multiple watersheds ("landscape scale"), river basins and even much larger swaths of the earth's surface. These scales are nested one within the other. Peter Berg and Raymond Dasmann coined the most widely cited definition of a bioregion; they describe it as referring to both a geographical terrain and a terrain of consciousness. In other words, the boundary that makes up a particular bioregion is not strictly determined by the lay of the land (i.e. its geography or biome). The bioregion also has a cultural dimension shaped by how people live in and identify with the place.[20] Bioregional boundaries, as defined by local inhabitants themselves, thus take a range of factors into account—most often including climate, topography, flora, fauna, soil and water together with the territory's socio-cultural characteristics, economy and human settlement patterns. Robert L. Thayer, Jr., a widely noted bioregional activist-scholar, aptly argues, "the bioregion is emerging as the most logical locus and scale for a sustainable, regenerative community to take root and to take place."[21]

The United States Geological Survey (USGS) is using watershed boundaries for its Border Environmental Health Initiative Regions project (see Figure 2). The USGS chose this delineation rather than the administrative boundary established by the 1983 La Paz agreement, which defines the border region as the area extending 100 kilometres north and 100 kilometres south of the international boundary line. The USGS rationale for this decision is that watersheds provide more meaningful and useful units of analysis when tackling transboundary socio-ecological challenges.

The Border Health Initiative Regions project has two main goals:

1. Develop and maintain a US–Mexico Border Transboundary Geographic Information System (GIS) and natural resource databases to help researchers, government officials, planners and concerned citizens to make decisions concerning the US–Mexico border region.
2. Investigate linkages between the condition of the physical environment and health including how environmental changes, contaminant trends, human and wildlife health interrelate.[22]

Bioregional initiatives conducted on national, binational and international scales do not necessarily advance the more challenging aspects of bioregionalism (e.g. authentic participatory democracy, communitarianism, subsidiarity, mutual aid). Yet national and international efforts are helping to reframe public discourse,

19. Raymond De Young and Thomas Princen, *The Localization Reader: Adapting to the Coming Downshift* (Cambridge, MA: MIT Press, 2012).

20. Peter Berg and Raymond Dasmann, "Reinhabiting California", *Ecologist*, Vol. 7 (1977), p. 8.

21. Robert L. Thayer, *Lifeplace: Bioregional Thought and Practice* (Berkeley, CA: University of California Press, 2003), p. 55.

22. US Geological Survey, "USGS US–Mexico Border Environmental Health Initiative", Web Mapping Application byFederal_User_Community, June 2013, available: <http://www.arcgis.com/home/item.html?id=496864a948ca4ed4a3ecccd0f24df2a7>(accessed 23 November 2013).

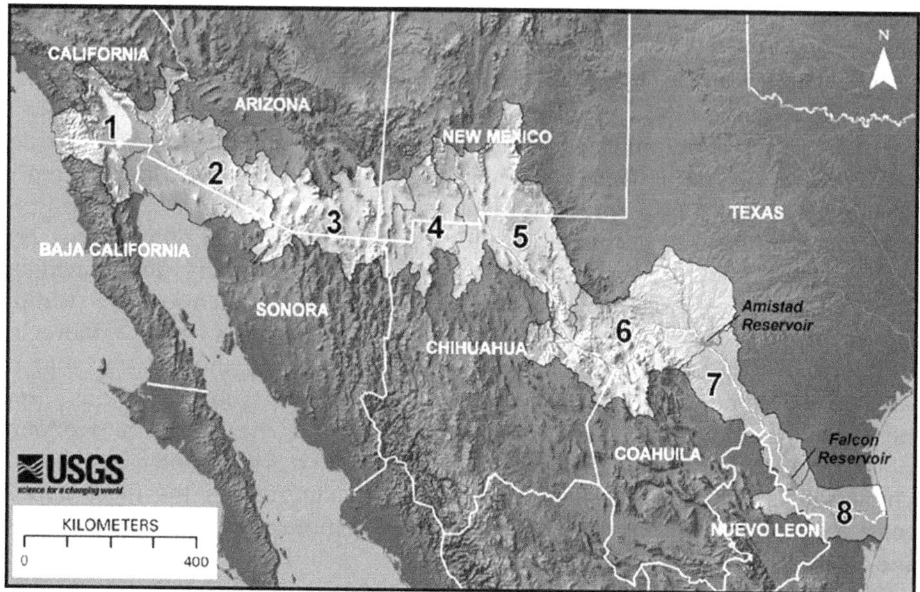

Figure 2. Eight Border Health Initiative Regions (Aligned along Watershed Boundaries) as Defined by the US Geological Survey.
Source: US Geological Survey, "Ecological Regions of the US–Mexico Border", *US–Mexico Border Environmental Health Initiative* (January 2011), available: <http://borderhealth.cr.usgs.gov/staticmaplib.html> (accessed 23 November 2013).

thereby creating new opportunities to advance bioregionalism's core commitments, including ecological restoration in urban and rural settings as well as in protected areas and working landscapes. This trend is evident in the 2013–2014 GNEB deliberations.[23]

The OBROH approach builds on bioregional theory and the work of those who have advocated "One *Border*/One Health" (OBOH). By intentionally integrating bioregional theory, principles of ecological restoration and One Health, the OBROH approach can help us get beyond two types of bias that constrain efforts to realise the kind of paradigm shift we need to bring about healthy place making and sustainability. The two biases are: (1) *metrocentric*—a fixation on cities in a way that ignores or undervalues the socio-ecological systems that interdependently bind urban and rural lifeplaces; and (2) *anthropocentric*—a failure to adequately take into account how human, animal and plant health are increasingly interconnected. The One Health paradigm acknowledges that human health is inseparable from the health of animals and the planet as a whole.[24]

23. The US–Mexico Good Neighbor Environmental Board has considered bioregional theory and practice in its current deliberations to improve ecological restoration along the border. Similarly, the Superfund Research Program of the US National Institute of Environmental Health Sciences (NIEHS) is supporting a transborder bioregional initiative led by the University of California, San Diego and Alter Terra, a binational non-governmental organisation.

24. Kelley Lee and Zabrina L. Brumme, "Operationalizing the One Health Approach: The Global Governance Challenges", *Health Policy and Planning*, Vol. 28, No. 7 (1 October 2013), pp. 778–785.

One Health in Theory and Practice

Those advocating a One Health perspective are quick to point out that humans, domestic animals, wildlife and plants are all interconnected with, and dependent on, the environment they inhabit. This idea of interconnectedness has recently gained recognition and popularity, but the idea goes back millennia. Human and animal health is affected, directly and indirectly, by the health of planetary ecosystems, which provide necessary food, air, water and protection.[25] Intact ecosystems play an important role in maintaining a diversity of species in balance and regulating the transmission of many infectious diseases. While human activity has impacted ecosystems for thousands of years, the past century has witnessed unprecedented rapid human population growth and economic development, driving extensive ecological changes and the emergence of both new and previously recognised infectious diseases. These activities include the encroachment into or destruction of wildlife habitat, agricultural land use changes, deforestation and habitat fragmentation, uncontrolled urbanisation, construction of dams and irrigation canals, release of chemical pollutants, intensive livestock production, climate changes, international travel and trade and human migration and settlement, as well as the emergence of new disease vectors, in the wake of increasingly globalised flows of life forms and other materials.

Over the past few decades, the emergence of human immunodeficiency virus (HIV), severe acute respiratory syndrome (SARS), H5N1 avian influenza, the 2009 H1N1 influenza pandemic and the re-emergence of extensively drug-resistant tuberculosis, dengue and cholera have clearly demonstrated the threat these global health challenges pose to health security. Quite recently, two additional novel viruses have emerged—the H7N9 influenza virus and Middle East Respiratory Syndrome Coronavirus (MERS-CoV)—causing concern to public health experts worldwide. In today's interconnected world, "in the context of infectious diseases, there is nowhere in the world from which we are remote and no one from whom we are disconnected."[26] Underlying this threat is the awareness that while the initial response to any infectious disease outbreak is primarily the responsibility of the domestic government, infectious diseases do not respect national borders and the failure of control measures in one country has the potential to put neighbouring countries and the health security of the entire world at risk. The spread of zoonotic diseases in the late 20th century and early 21st century has inspired a new discipline known as "Global Health." Global Health approaches environmental public health as a transborder phenomenon and thus fits well within the OBROH narrative presented here.

Recognising the globalisation of health risks, and the threat of bioterrorism post 9/11 following the anthrax letters, the US Assistant Secretary of Preparedness and Response funded the Early Warning Infectious Disease Surveillance (EWIDS) Program in 2003 to build early warning systems to detect both intentional and natural disease threats along US international borders. The overarching goal of EWIDS was to improve cross-border early warning of infectious diseases in North America and build the capacity of public health systems in the US border

---

25. Patz et al., *op. cit.*

26. Institute of Medicine (US) Committee on Emerging Microbial Threats to Health, "Preface", in J. Ledergerg, R.E. Shope and S.C. Oaks (eds.), *Emerging Infections: Microbial Threats to Health in the United States* (Washington, DC: National Academies Press, 1992), p. v.

states with a focus on infectious disease with a major public health impact (e.g. bioterrorism agents, emerging and re-emerging pathogens, pandemic influenza). Critical to EWIDS' success in addressing the complexities of cross-border disease outbreaks was close collaboration with public health partners in neighbouring border states and coordination of efforts to detect and respond more effectively to infectious disease threats.

The California–Baja California border region encompasses a wide range of ecosystems, topography, dense urban areas and agricultural developments that coexist in a limited geographic area and create numerous human–animal–environmental interfaces. These interfaces pose a significant risk to animal, human, environmental and plant health, as evidenced by frequent wildlife die-offs, antibiotic-resistant bacteria in streams, beach closures due to faecal contamination, pesticide toxicities, zoonotic infectious disease outbreaks and vector-borne diseases.[27] With the increasing awareness that prompt detection, diagnosis and response to newly emerging infectious diseases requires working outside of traditional disciplinary silos and forging new multi-sectoral partnerships, and the recognition of the marked absence of any organisation comprehensively addressing the health risks posed by these complex interfaces, EWIDS founded One Border/One Health (OBOH) in June 2011. This effort connected individuals representing multiple sectors in the California–Baja California region in order to address emerging diseases, risk factors contributing to the region's susceptibility, and actions to monitor and intervene such as establishing joint animal–human surveillance systems for early warning of emerging infectious diseases. Cooperating across both jurisdictional and sectorial boundaries and the formation of groups such as the OBOH are critical to creating sustainable solutions to health risks at the human–animal–environmental interface and building resilient communities.[28]

The OBOH was successful in encouraging scholars and practitioners to work collaboratively in order to establish a process for (1) enhancing surveillance for emerging and re-emerging pathogens using the One Health concept, (2) developing mechanisms for data collection and exchange among stakeholders, and (3) raising community awareness to integrate the One Health concept in education and training.[29] Table 1 summarises key features of the One Border/One Health

27. An example of this can be seen in the re-emergence of tuberculosis cases in the form of Multi-Drug Resistant Tuberculosis (MDR-TB). This is a major global threat that significantly affects US border cities including San Diego, which suffers double the national US average prevalence of MDR-TB. See World Health Organization, "Multidrug-Resistant Tuberculosis (MDR-TB)", October 2013, available: <http://www.who.int/tb/challenges/mdr/en/> (accessed 25 November 2013); Betsy McKay, "Risk of Deadly TB Exposure Grows along US–Mexico Border", 8 March 2013, available <http://online.wsj.com/news/articles/SB10001424127887323293704578336283658347240> (accessed 25 November 2013). Also see Robert Donnelly, *Our Shared Border: Success Stories in US–Mexico Collaboration* (Washington, DC: Border Research Partnership/Woodrow Wilson International Center for Scholars, January 2012); and M.F. Moreau et al., "Selenium, Arsenic, DDT and Other Contaminants in Four Fish Species in the Salton Sea, California, Their Temporal Trends, and Their Potential Impact on Human Consumers and Wildlife", *Lake and Reservoir Management*, Vol. 23 (2007), pp. 536–569.

28. One Border One Health, *A California-Baja California Regional Network*, available: <http://www.oneborderonehealth.com/> (accessed 23 November 2013).

29. The progress of these collaborative efforts has been presented at numerous professional conferences including presentations at the Second International One Health Conference; the International Society for Disease Surveillance Annual Conference; the Dynamics of Preparedness Conference; the National Environmental Health Association Annual Conference; the National Hispanic Medical Association Resident Leadership Program; the General Meeting of the American Society for Microbiology; and

Table 1. Key Features of One Bioregion/One Health.

Key Feature	Benefit
Transborder	• Facilitates bioregional planning through integrated watershed management • Improves surveillance and response to health threats • Improves binational communication
Holistic	• Refocuses disease-centred approach with a proactive, wellness, system-based approach • Shifts from species-specific to multiple species/habitat conservation and restoration approaches • Values human health, animal health and the environment • Examines how place-based physical, economic and social characteristics interact
Multi-disciplinary and Cross-sectoral collaboration	• Creates a culture of interdependence • Disrupts traditional silos; designs interventions for collective impact • Shares knowledge, best practices and protocols • Creates synergy among different institutional perspectives and experiences • Promotes flexible and rapid responses to threats • Integrates diverse forms of knowledge and action through multisector, multiscale and multidisciplinary collaboration (3Ms).
Transparency in processes and decision making	• Builds trust-based relationships and legitimacy • Encourages data sharing • Optimises resources and efforts
Platform for information exchange and discussion	• Improves communication and sharing of ideas • Creates a network linking distributed intelligence • Leverages the power of spatial analytics, visualisation and multimedia
Effective champions, sponsors and formal leadership positions (co-chairs)	• Ensures objectives are met • Access to resources and networks • Ability to influence other organisations • High level of active participation • Builds legitimacy
Cross-cultural understanding	• Seeks common ground • Culturally appropriate strategies
Chatham House Rules	• Encourages free discussion • High level of active participation
Participation of federal and state actors	• Fosters political will and high-level support
Collaborative binational committees	• Directs interactive problem solving • Creates the opportunity for bioregional planning • Builds capabilities for inter-sectoral collaboration • Creates a common vocabulary

Continued

Table 1. Continued.

Key Feature	Benefit
Training, education and outreach	• Increases community awareness • Provides community with bioregional information • Builds workforce capacity • Aids in recruitment of new members and partner organisations
Evaluation of collaborative process	• Identifies strengths and weaknesses in collaborative process • Informs continuous initiative evolution and improvement • Improves retention of membership
Bioregional scale	• Creates a contextual understanding and focus on local humans and animals and their social and ecological environment • Improves flexibility, resilience, adaptability and timely responsiveness at the local and bioregional scale • Relates place-based health planning to ecosystem management

approach. The table uses the term "One Bioregion" as opposed to "One Border" in its title to emphasise the place-based nature of the relationship, including the value added by the new politics of bioregionally oriented healthy city planning.

One Health in Global Perspective

In addition to North America, the value of collaborative cross-border regional networks has been demonstrated in other areas of the world. The Human Animal Infections and Risk Surveillance (HAIRS) is a government-funded multi-agency and cross-disciplinary horizon-scanning group covering England, Wales, Scotland and Northern Ireland.[30] The group has met every month since 2004 and acts as a forum to identify and assess infections with potential for interspecies transfer that may pose a risk to animal or human health. The countries around the Mediterranean Sea started the EpiSouth Project in 2006, as a framework for collaboration for communicable disease surveillance and training among 26 participating countries from southern Europe, the Balkans, North Africa and the Middle East as well as several international organisations.[31] The EpiSouth Project is a valuable demonstration that even regions in conflict and with difficult borders can form effective partnerships, find common ground and engage in commitments to promote health security.

One Health has expanded beyond its initial primary concern with zoonotics (i.e. diseases caused by pathogens that can be transmitted between animals and

the NORTHCOM One Health: Environmental Health Considerations for Global Emerging Infectious Disease and Illness Conference.

30. A.L. Walsh and D. Morgan, "Identifying Hazards, Assessing the Risks", *The Veterinary Record*, Vol. 157 (2005), pp. 684–687.

31. M.G. Dente et al., "EpiSouth: A Network for Communicable Disease Control in the Mediterranean Region and the Balkans", *Euro Surveill*, Vol. 14, No. 5 (2009), pp. 1–4.

humans) to include food- and water-borne disease, the health effects of global climate change, and the risks of environmental toxins and chronic conditions such as cancer, obesity and aging.[32] This expanded approach to the initial One Health agenda can be seen in new calls for research proposals. For instance, the USA's National Science Foundation (NSF) is encouraging research on the ecological, evolutionary and socio-ecological principles and processes that influence the transmission dynamics of infectious diseases. The NSF issued a call for proposals seeking projects that focus on "... the determinants and interactions of transmission among humans, non-human animals, and/or plants. This includes, for example, the spread of pathogens; the influence of environmental factors such as climate; the population dynamics and genetics of reservoir species or hosts; or the cultural, social, behavioral, and economic dimensions of disease transmission."[33] This type of research interrelates spatial scales by taking into account local–global flows and networks as well as systems and structures.[34] Leadership development, training and new forms of education and governance are important elements of such efforts.[35]

Leadership, Training and Workforce Development

Regional public health and environmental challenges require a unified strategy to ensure well-designed and mutually agreed upon disease surveillance and response protocols, care coordination for binational patients, and integrated prevention and health promotion messaging. Policies are developed by leaders at the local, state and federal levels and require accurate information, careful deliberation, negotiation and consideration of environmental and health impacts. Binational collaboration is constantly evolving, especially considering government transitions, organisational workforce shifts and new styles of leadership (e.g. community leadership), and within this progression it is vital that leaders seek opportunities for authentic civic engagement that will lead to positive change. One way this can be achieved is through understanding of cross-border regional governance, leadership development and binational training programmes to support the development of a qualified workforce equipped to deal with the challenges of this unique space.

Leadership in cross-border health planning is inherently tied to protocols of communication, and awareness of policies, rules and regulations. In the California–Baja California border region, informal and formal transnational networks exist, encompassing non-profit organisations, universities, government and health care

32. Lee and Brumme, *op. cit.*, p. 5; Margalit Younger, Heather R. Morrow-Almeida, Stephen M. Vindigni and Andrew L. Dannenberg, "The Built Environment, Climate Change, and Health: Opportunities for Co-Benefits", *American Journal of Preventive Medicine*, Vol. 35 (2008), pp. 517–526.

33. National Science Foundation, "Ecology and Evolution of Infectious Diseases (EEID)", Program Solicitation NSF 13-577 (November 2013), available: <http://www.nsf.gov/pubs/2013/nsf13577/nsf13577.htm> (accessed 5 September 2014).

34. On flows, see, for example, Gert Spaargaren, A.P.J. Mol and Frederick H. Buttel, *Governing Environmental Flows: Global Challenges to Social Theory* (Cambridge, MA: MIT Press, 2006). For network theory, see, for example, Michele-Lee Moore and Frances Westley, "Surmountable Chasms: Networks and Social Innovation for Resilient Systems", *Ecology and Society*, Vol. 16 (2011), available: <http://www.ecologyandsociety.org/vol16/iss1/art5/> (accessed 26 June 2014).

35. William Clark, "Sustainability Science: A Room of Its Own", *Proceedings of the National Academy of Sciences*, Vol. 104 (2007), pp. 1737–1738.

agencies to address shared concerns. While both states operate under federal mandates and policies, these rules are often adapted to meet the unique needs of the local and complex border communities. For example, the California–Baja California region has the highest number of tuberculosis (TB) cases in both countries. At the local level, public health departments on both sides work closely to ensure care continuity for every binational, mobile individual living with TB, including those with multi-drug-resistant TB. Local health departments report new TB cases to the state to ensure accurate case counting (in Mexico this process also facilitates access to various treatment options).

Adequately addressing the needs of a border community requires effective transnational communication, beginning at the local level and then possibly involving regional and/or state government, depending on the protocol within that country.[36] Within the US public health system, solutions to public health issues are managed by the local health department, with the support of the state public health department and local community partners, while involving federal partners when necessary.[37] In Mexico, under the direction of the National Secretariat of Health, the state secretariats of health oversee all local and state public health efforts and policies. Understanding the structure and functions of government agencies on both sides of the border, especially differences between the US and Mexico, is necessary to manoeuvre within each system and achieve the desired outcomes.

The US and Mexico have a long history of collaborating on epidemiologic events including infectious disease outbreaks, care management of binational patients, public health laboratory coordination and other issues affecting binational populations. However, there is still a desire for better electronic systems for sharing information and formalising cooperative agreements to facilitate regional collaboration.[38] The *Technical Guidelines for United States–Mexico Coordination on Public Health Events of Mutual Interest* aim to improve communication pathways.[39] Public health agencies in the USA and Mexico are often required to communicate with their agency at the same level in the opposite country (i.e. local–local, state–state or federal–federal). Timely sharing of information is critical. Currently dissemination and training on the guidelines presents a significant challenge and it will take time before reaching full implementation.[40]

36. Cecilie Modvar and Gilberto C. Gallopín, *Report of the Workshop, Sustainable Development: Epistemological Challenges to Science and Technology* (Santiago, Chile: United Nations, CEPAL, 2004).

37. C. Denman et al., *Working beyond Borders: A Handbook for Transborder Projects in Health* (Hermosillo, Sonora, Mexico: El Colegio de Sonora, 2004); M. Zúñiga, "Border Health", in Sana Loue and Martha Sajatovic (eds.), *Encyclopedia of Immigrant Health* (New York: Springer, 2012), pp. 299–305.

38. Zúñiga, *op. cit.*

39. These Guidelines were developed in 2004 by the Core Group on Epidemiologic Surveillance of the Health Working Group, U.S. –Mexico Binational Commission and subsequently refined by the U.S. Centers for Disease Control and Prevention (CDC), Department of Health and Human Services (HHS) and by the General Directorate of Epidemiology (DGE), Secretaria de Salud (SSA), Mexico. They can be downloaded at <http://www.cdph.ca.gov/programs/cobbh/Documents/GuidelineforUS-MexicoEventCoordination.pdf>.

40. Mexico's Ministry of Health and the Centers for Disease Control and Prevention are currently establishing a "US-Mexico Binational Communication Pathways Protocol" to facilitate disease-specific, timely and appropriate communication channels. In one study that examined the efficacy of this new communication pathway, the authors conclude that "[b]inational notifications using the pilot communication protocol improve documentation of binational morbidity. In addition, results from pilot participation suggest that binational reporting is both feasible and beneficial to communication between

Transborder networks are necessary to create knowledge-action groups to enable cross-border communication and governance. One successful group in the California–Baja California region is the Border Health Consortium of California—a member-driven and cross-disciplinary binational initiative that meets regularly to discuss border health issues, network, disseminate information and explore opportunities for collaboration. Traditionally, many of these cross-border collaborations have been informal, but there is a growing interest in institutionalising partnerships to encourage sustainable and coordinated responses to public health events.

It is widely recognised that there is a need to train individuals working in the border region to create a culturally competent workforce. A growing practice to promote cross-jurisdictional collaboration is the implementation of binational training programmes, involving cross-border and interdisciplinary teamwork among trainees (both professionals and students), experiential field work opportunities, and public health and medical student interactions in both countries. These programmes allow students to directly work together across borders and with communities on both sides of the border, while making significant contributions and developing practical skills (e.g. research skills). An example of this type of binational collaborative training model is the Fogarty International-supported AIDS International Training Research Program.[41]

Participants in the Fogarty programme are able to take classes, receive co-mentoring at collaborating institutions and acquire experience in the field of the partnering country, as well as take advantage of opportunities to engage in long-distance learning through different technological modalities. Participants gain a deeper understanding of systems and cultural differences, which is essential in creating a culturally competent workforce. Also, investing resources locally, by training students and workers rooted in the region, creates more resilient communities.

Another example of a binational collaborative training programme is VIIDAI (Viajes Interinstitucional de Integración Docente, Asistencial y de Investigación), a partnership between California and Baja California universities.[42] The VIIDAI programme is designed for medical students, public health graduate students and faculty, from both sides of the border, to work collaboratively on public health projects in under-served communities. Participants visit colonias, which are small farming towns lacking basic infrastructure, in Baja California. In collaboration with community leaders, they address concerns and offer solutions. Activities commonly include providing medical and dental services, as well as conducting community needs assessments and health promotion projects. It is a rewarding experience for participants as they learn about global health issues and have the opportunity to work with a multidisciplinary team, learning from leaders, community members as well

public health partners" (Andrew Thorton et al., "US–Mexico Binational Infectious Disease Case and Outbreak Notification Communication Pathway Pilot", June 2013, available: <https://cste.confex.com/cste/2013/webprogram/Paper1755.html> [accessed 23 November 2013]).

41. The Fogarty programme is a US–Mexico cross-border training opportunity in HIV, TB and STI prevention and is coordinated by two of the largest universities in the region, the University of California, San Diego (UCSD) and Universidad Autónoma de Baja California (Autonomous University of Baja California), with involvement from several partnering institutions including the US–Mexico Border Health Commission and the Colegio de la Frontera Norte (México's College of the Northern Border).

42. VIIDAI is a partnership between San Diego State University, UCSD and Universidad Autónoma de Baja California.

as their peers, and develop skills in cultural competency. It is an advantageous combination of academic, cultural and binational collaboration training.

A third and final example of a binational collaborative training programme involves civically engaged research led by Alter Terra (a binational non-governmental organisation [NGO]), the University of California, San Diego (UCSD) Superfund Research Center (SRC), the Center for US–Mexican Studies, and the Universidad Autonoma de Baja California (UABC). Alter Terra, UCSD and UABC designed and implemented a large-scale environmental public health assessment in one of Tijuana's rapidly urbanising canyons called Los Laureles. Over the past decade, the seven mile stretch of Los Laureles Canyon grew in numbers from practically 0 to 70,000 people, many of whom lack basic urban services (e.g. a functioning sewer system, trash collection, paved roads). As is the case in many of Tijuana's canyons, Los Laureles has numerous unregulated dumpsites, containing wastes from diverse sources (e.g. hospitals, industry, construction, households). Los Laureles Canyon has a south-to-north topographical tilt to it as part of the Tijuana River Watershed, so although it lies in Tijuana, Mexico, all drainage through the canyon flows across the US–Mexico border into the USA. During the spring of 2013, UCSD and UABC faculty, researchers and students, assisted by Alter Terra, carried out 388 face-to-face interviews in targeted neighbourhoods of Los Laureles.[43]

The survey asked questions about demographics, water hygiene and sanitation, health-related discomforts and symptoms, disease history, public safety and services, and access to medical care. It is the first stage in a long-term epidemiological plan to causally link exposure to toxicants with health outcomes. The effort is motivated by the working hypothesis that exposures to hazardous substances (e. g. in contaminated air, water, land, plants, animals) are taking place and causing negative health impacts, not only among the canyon's residents living in close proximity to the dumps, but also downstream in human and biotic communities on the US side of the border.

Leadership and Health Diplomacy

Training public health professionals in the area of global health diplomacy and cooperation is a critical step in bringing leaders together from both countries to work alongside one another. Health diplomacy is defined as "the chosen method of interaction between stakeholders engaged in public health and politics for the purpose of representation, cooperation, resolving disputes, improving health systems, and securing the right to health for vulnerable populations."[44] There are currently no standards for training in health diplomacy.

Programmes such as *Leaders Across Borders/Líderes Atraves de la Frontera* aim to address this very issue through training public health professionals on how to work collaboratively binationally. Specifically, *Leaders Across Borders* is a 10-

43. The survey of 388 households was completed under the direction of co-PIs Wael Al-Delaimy, MD, PhD (UCSD) and Keith Pezzoli, PhD (UCSD), together with Mexico-based collaborative partner Rufino Menchaca Díaz, MD, MPH, PhD (UABC). Thirty graduate students from UABC got the training they needed to do the survey, which they successfully did, door to door, assisted by UABC faculty researchers and leaders of Alter Terra, namely Oscar Romo and Jennifer Hazard.

44. Kelley Lee and Richard Smith, "What is 'Global Health Diplomacy'? A Conceptual Review", *Global Health Governance*, Vol. V. No. I (Fall 2011), pp. 1–12, available: <http://www.ghgj.org> (accessed 25 November 2013).

month programme that teaches and mentors health professionals and community leaders to design and implement projects to address the needs of under-served communities in the US–Mexico border region.[45] Participants learn how to effectively collaborate with one another by developing skills in health diplomacy and also gaining a deeper understanding of cultural differences and binational health care systems. Participants navigate the challenging binational collaboration process, finding solutions to language and communication barriers, institutional and cultural differences, and resource imbalances.

Community Knowledge in Civically Engaged Research

No one better understands a community's needs than those living, breathing and working within it. Researchers and programme directors are learning that it is essential to engage members prior to project conception to ensure the services are tailored to community realities and needs and in order to increase the likelihood of programme success. This requires new forms of science communication. Significant attention is now being focused on the call to transform institutions of higher education from ivory towers into ivory bridges.[46] The intent is to create "engaged universities" (i.e., knowledge institutions rooted in their region where use-inspired, problem-solving, solutions-oriented research has as much value as more traditional basic research).[47] The engaged university movement can significantly advance the OBROH approach in theory and practice.

A university's role in society is shifting in the face of globalisation and heightened competitiveness worldwide among nations and city-regions. On the one hand, some university leaders and scholars advocate the corporatisation of the academy following a conservative ethos focused on commercialisation. This stems in part from the increasing stress being placed on universities to enhance regional innovation and competitiveness "via harnessing the economic benefit of science and knowledge, in which the sub-national scale plays an important role."[48] On the other hand, some university leaders and scholars aim to make the academy more accountable from social justice and equity standpoints involving critical pedagogy and civically engaged research and service learning. These two types of engagement are not necessarily mutually exclusive. Harloe and Perry argue that these trajectories constitute a mixed bag including opportunities and threats embodied in conflicts over the university's mission, internal culture, governance and allocation of resources.[49]

The Superfund Research Center (SRC) at UCSD is one example where the effort to advance civically engaged research is happening. The SRC is integrating

45. The US–Mexico Border Health Commission; the Arizona Department of Health Services, Office of Border Health; the University of Arizona Mel and Enid Zuckerman College of Public Health; the México Secretariat of Health; and the Colegios de la Frontera Norte y Sonora support this novel programme.

46. Gerhard Sonnert and Gerald James Holton, *Ivory Bridges: Connecting Science and Society* (Cambridge, MA: MIT Press, 2002).

47. David Watson, *The Engaged University: International Perspectives on Civic Engagement, International Studies in Higher Education* (New York: Routledge, 2011).

48. Michael Harloe and Beth Perry, "Universities, Localities and Regional Development: The Emergence of the 'Mode 2' University?", *International Journal of Urban and Regional Research*, Vol. 28 (2004), pp. 212–223.

49. *Ibid.*

community knowledge and research through a bioregional approach.[50] Taking into account goals spelled out by the US Environmental Protection Agency (EPA) Border 2020 Program and the GNEB, the UCSD SRC has focused on sites on both sides of the US–Mexico border. The focus in Mexico has been on Los Laureles Canyon, a seven mile stretch of canyon land in the Tijuana River Watershed.[51] In the US, the UCSD SRC has focused on San Diego's Pueblo Watershed contaminated by diffuse sources of pollution.[52]

A Forward-Looking Perspective

As the World Health Organization points out, health is not the mere absence of disease: "Health is a state of complete physical, mental and social well-being and not merely the absence of disease or infirmity."[53] Many aspects of health are related to socio-economic status or mental and psychological well-being even in the absence of disease. For instance, health quality is partly determined by the degree to which one enjoys a secure sense of attachment to a safe and convivial life-place (i.e. rootedness). From this perspective, it is fruitful to join bioregional theory and practice with the insights and institutional advances made by One Health advocates. The OBROH narrative helps draw attention to the 21st century's socio-ecological stresses and the concomitant need to better align political economy and ecology. Such an alignment is crucial to the challenge of establishing healthy place-based planning that can cultivate just, resilient and sustainable communities. A number of trajectories are worth noting here: advances in environmental epidemiology, telecoupling and the articulation of bioregional justice as a new ethical framework linking health and ecosystems.

Environmental Epidemiology

Contaminants flowing through the environment do not recognise borders. Likewise, disease vectors are not easily shut down at border checkpoints; disease knows no border. All of this is forcing public health officials, academicians and researchers to think differently about how to address human health. The science of environmental

50. UCSD's SRC, in place since 2000 and recently funded for another five years (to 2017), is generating new perspectives on the molecular and genetic basis of toxicant exposure, leading to new methodologies for gauging health risks and assessing health effects—especially among vulnerable populations living under cumulative stresses associated with poverty. The SRC's Community Engagement Core is tasked with linking the SRC's science to real world applications that benefit vulnerable communities. This creates opportunities for faculty as well as graduate and undergraduate students to link science to policy and planning in distressed areas on both sides of the US–Mexico border. The Community Engagement Core aims to advance bioregional justice and sustainability in the San Diego–Tijuana city-region by enabling students, civically engaged researchers, community leaders and a diverse range of professionals to collaborate across academic and jurisdictional boundaries.

51. See Keith Pezzoli, Shannon Bradley, Laura Castenada and Hiram Sarabia, *Los Laureles Canyon: Research in Action* (a 28 minute UCSD-TV documentary focused on the water/climate/poverty nexus in human settlements along the US–Mexico border) (November 2009), available: <http://www.ucsd.tv/loslaureles/>.

52. See <http://superfund.ucsd.edu/initiative/brownfieldsvacant-lot-asset-mapping-survey>.

53. Preamble to the Constitution of the World Health Organization as adopted by the International Health Conference, New York, 19–22 June 1946; signed on 22 July 1946 by the representatives of 61 States and entered into force on 7 April 1948. Available: <http://www.who.int/about/definition/en/print.html> (accessed 16 April 2014).

epidemiology will likely become more important over coming decades. Environmental epidemiology, as defined by the National Cancer Institute (USA), "seeks to understand how physical, chemical, biologic, as well as social and economic factors affect human health. Social factors—or in other words where one lives, works, socializes, or buys food—often influence exposure to environmental factors."[54]

Telecoupling

Studies that attempt to correlate toxicant exposures with health outcomes in particular places must grapple with issues of scale posed by globalisation. The nature of this challenge is captured by the concept of telecoupling. Telecoupling, as described by Jianguo Liu et al., is an umbrella concept that refers to socio-economic and environmental interactions over distances.[55] The telecoupling concept is an outgrowth of Coupled Human And Natural Systems (CHANS) research, which has been concentrating on human–nature interactions within particular places. The unit of analysis in telecoupling research is not a discrete place; rather it is relationships among places (i.e. human–nature interactions in the space of flows that interdependently bind the fate of people and places across distances).[56] At its 98th annual meeting in 2013, the Ecological Society of America held a symposium focused on "Ecological Sustainability in a Telecoupled World." Enthusiasts of the telecoupling framework (with its emphasis on CHANS, flows, agents, causes and effects) spelled out its benefits:

> The framework can help to analyze system components and their interrelationships, identify research gaps, detect hidden costs and untapped benefits, provide a useful means to incorporate feedbacks as well as trade-offs and synergies across multiple systems (sending, receiving, and spillover systems), and improve the understanding of distant interactions and the effectiveness of policies for socioeconomic and environmental sustainability from local to global levels.[57]

Bioregional Justice

Human exploitation of the earth's stocks and flows of natural capital brings up issues of global and bioregional justice. Bioregional justice shares the concerns of environmental justice, but does so in a way that also highlights ecosystems as common good assets, and human–nature relations as manifest in human settlement patterns at a regional scale. Bioregional justice thus integrates multiple layers of justice (e.g. social, economic, environmental, global) by advancing a unifying place-based approach to improving the land, ecosystems and urban–rural relationships in a particular bioregion. Bioregional justice ensures that the benefits, opportunities and risks arising from creating, operating and living in a territorially

54. National Cancer Institute, "Environmental Epidemiology", available: <http://epi.grants.cancer.gov/environmental/> (accessed 23 November 2013).

55. Jianguo Liu et al., "Framing Sustainability in a Telecoupled World", *Ecology and Society*, Vol. 18, No. 2 (2011), pp. 1–19.

56. *Ibid.*

57. *Ibid.*

bounded network of human settlements (i.e. a bioregion where urban–rural–wildland spaces co-evolve socially, culturally and ecologically) are shared equitably through healthy relationships and secure place-based attachments. Bioregional justice seeks equity and fairness in how a bioregion's assets—including nature's sources, sinks and ecosystems needed for life and living—are accessed, utilised and sustainably conserved for current and future generations.

Bioregional justice is a normative theory at the heart of the OBROH narrative. Bioregional justice elevates the visibility and significance of ethics with respect to community health and land. Aldo Leopold's land ethic resonates here: "A thing is right when it tends to preserve the integrity, stability, and beauty of the biotic community. It is wrong when it tends otherwise."[58] Leopold understood that land is more than soil; it is "a fountain of energy flowing through a circuit of soils, plants, and animals."[59] The land ethic (like OBROH) "enlarges the boundaries of the community to include soils, waters, plants, and animals, or collectively: the land."[60] Establishing an ethic to realise bioregional justice (i.e. a place-based ecopolity where fairness and healthy resilience prevails in how we relate with one another *and* with the land, waters, habitat, plants and animals upon which we depend) is not just an ecological challenge; it is also a socio-political, economic, cultural and aesthetic challenge. The great urban and regional visionary Lewis Mumford stated this view poignantly over three-quarters of a century ago (a perspective as relevant today as it was then): "The re-animation and re-building of regions, as deliberate works of collective art, is the grand task of politics for the coming generation."[61]

Conclusion

OBROH is an integrative approach that aims to improve human and environmental health through knowledge networking, ecosystem management, community participation in science–society relations, leadership development and cross-disciplinary training. OBROH is redefining how we understand human–nature relationships in the quest for healthy place making. But there is a long way to go. Linking local and bioregional/global information in a pragmatic manner is a major challenge. For instance, as local entities undertake urban ecological restoration projects, it would help if they knew how their efforts fit into larger, bioregional ecological restoration efforts and activities (e.g., could the use of multiple vacant lots for community-based urban agriculture and rainwater harvesting within a particular watershed be configured in such a way that it adds value to food and water security on a bioregional scale?). Three science–society gaps thwart the equitable co-production, access and use of knowledge necessary to address questions of this sort. The three gaps are:

1. Epistemic (gaps within and between formal and informal knowledge ecosystems)
2. Analytical (gaps between global, regional and local scale data)
3. Socio-economic (gap between those with technical resources and those without)

58. Aldo Leopold, "The Land Ethic", in A. Light and H. Rolston III (eds.), *Environmental Ethics* (Oxford: Blackwell, 2003), p. 39.

59. *Ibid.*

60. *Ibid.*

61. Lewis Mumford, *The Culture of Cities* (London: Routledge/Thoemmes, 1977), p. 348.

Narrowing these gaps requires new socio-technical systems (using big data informatics, visualisation and mapping techniques) that can illuminate how built environments, ecosystems and health interact across spatial and temporal scales. Narrowing these gaps also depends on an active civil society including mutually reinforcing community–university engagement and equitable public–private partnerships that can generate new types of use-inspired, solutions-oriented research and action. OBROH is an emergent approach that seeks this kind of engagement and partnership building—especially in the context of enabling ecological restoration and healthy place making that is sustainable and resilient.

Funding and Acknowledgements

The US National Institute of Environmental Health Sciences (NIEHS) of the National Institutes of Health (NIH) under Award Number P42ES010337 supported some of the research reported in this article. The content is solely the responsibility of the authors and does not necessarily represent the official views of the NIEHS, NIH or any of the other agencies to which the co-authors have affiliation.

The Cross-Border Metropolis in a Global Age: A Conceptual Model and Empirical Evidence from the US–Mexico and European Border Regions

LAWRENCE A. HERZOG and CHRISTOPHE SOHN

In a globalising urban world, cross-border metropolises are important spatial configurations that reflect the interplay between the space of flows and the space of places. This article scrutinises the different logics at play as urbanisation occurs around international boundaries. It disentangles the contradictory "bordering dynamics" that shape cross-border urban spaces in the context of globalisation and territorial restructuring. Because national borders embody multifaceted as well as ambivalent roles and meanings, they can be viewed as critical barometers for understanding how globalisation impacts cross-border metropolitan space. The first two sections of the article explore the two globalisation processes—"debordering" and "rebordering"—that define the formation of cross-border metropolises. We view the border as a social and political construction; as such, we propose a conceptual framework that addresses the changing role and significance of boundaries in the making of cross-border metropolises. Finally, we offer two contrasting empirical case studies, one from the US–Mexico border, the other from a European border region. By studying bordering dynamics in San Diego–Tijuana and Geneva, we are able to draw some conclusions about the challenges faced by cross-border metropolitan spaces as well as some mechanisms that will govern their future organisation.

Introduction

Globalisation in the twenty first century is leading to new forms of spatial relations, including the emerging prototype of the "global city."[1] The gradual acceleration of transnational banking, offshore manufacturing, multination trade blocs, global communications, digital technology and the international division of labour have all shaped a profound "internationalisation" of urban space. No longer are cities merely artefacts shaped by local stakeholders; urban centres have become containers increasingly developed and transformed by international actors, from corporate investors and transnational financial interests to transborder marketing entities and cross-national governmental organisations. To accommodate the forces of globalisation, the city has been forced to reinvent itself; sprawling "edge cities" and dense,

1. Saskia Sassen, *The Global City: New York, London, Tokyo* (Princeton, NJ: Princeton University Press, 2001).

high-tech corporate business districts are just two recent responses to the globalisation of the metropolis.

Globalisation has also shifted urban populations towards international boundaries, leading to the need for a discourse on these new globalising urban spaces, or what one might term "transfrontier metropolises."[2] Following the rise of the nation-state in the nineteenth century, cities usually evolved in locations entirely inside (and often distant from) the boundaries of sovereign nations. Yet during the late twentieth century, this pattern began to loosen in some regions across the planet, as population, economic resources and infrastructure migrated towards the edges of nations, leading to the formation of city regions that sprawl across international boundaries, notably in Europe and North America.[3]

The evolution of transfrontier metropolitan regions remains a very recent phenomenon if one looks at the historic relationship between cities and territorial boundaries. Historically, the location and growth of cities has been controlled and managed by nation-states. Territorial politics in the nineteenth and early twentieth centuries dictated that nations guard their borders. This "shelter" mentality fostered a common pattern of settlement in which the largest urban concentrations tended to be located away from the physical edges of a nation.[4] Before 1950, in fact, border regions were viewed as buffer zones that helped to protect the nation from invasion by land. Under these conditions, there were few significant cities near national boundaries. A glance at the map of Western Europe corroborates this: Paris, Madrid, Rome and Frankfurt all lie in the interior of their respective countries. Across the Atlantic in the Americas, we see a similar pattern: Mexico City, Lima, São Paulo or Bogota are all a considerable distance from the nearest international boundary. Only in the second half of the last century does one begin to see cases where border territory evolves into prime real estate for settlement and city building. The age of land warfare across much of the planet is over, although there are, of course, conflict zones that remain. Meanwhile, global markets and free trade are the new dominant realities. We have entered a new global age where property at the edges of nations can attract investors, businesses and governments. Industrial parks, highways, rail systems and airports that once bypassed international frontiers are relocating there. It is now possible for large cities to be developed along international frontiers.

In this article, we conceive cross-border metropolises as urban configurations that can potentially benefit from the interplay between the flows of globalisation (space of flows) and the proximity of territorial borders (space of places). We recognise that open borders offer opportunities for cross-border metropolises to reinforce their position at the heart of global economic networks and to affirm

2. Lawrence A. Herzog, "Cross-National Urban Structure in the Era of Global Cities: The US–Mexico Transfrontier Metropolis", *Urban Studies*, Vol. 28, No. 4 (1991), pp. 519–533.

3. Important European transfrontier urban agglomerations, with populations ranging from several hundred thousand to more than one million are found along the Swiss–French–German border, the Dutch–German–Belgian border, in metropolitan Geneva on the Swiss–French border and in metropolitan Strasbourg on the French–German border. In North America, one finds transfrontier urban regions of between half a million and five million people along the Canada–US border and along the Mexico–US border at Tijuana–San Diego, Ciudad Juarez–El Paso and other urbanised zones.

4. See also Lawrence A. Herzog, *Where North Meets South* (Austin, TX: CMAS/University of Texas Press, 1990), pp. 2–4, 13–17.

their autonomy as cross-border regional entities.[5] Yet the process of what we term "debordering," which allowed cross-border metropolises to mobilise the border as a resource, has been countered by what we call "rebordering" trends, notably via the post-9/11 securitisation discourse. If both debordering and rebordering are seen as emerging processes embedded in the globalisation of space,[6] their combined impact on cross-border metropolises calls for further investigation. How do these contradictory dynamics (re)structure the social, economic and political relations that shape cross-border metropolitan spaces? To what extent does rebordering challenge the future of cross-border metropolises? How can we conceptualise the debordering vs. rebordering dynamic for cross-border conurbations?

With these research questions in mind, the aim of this article is to investigate the ways in which cross-border metropolises are affected by contradictory dynamics. Because borders conspicuously embody multifaceted as well as ambivalent roles and meanings, they appear to be critical barometers for understanding how globalisation impacts cross-border metropolises. In the first two sections of the article, we explore the two globalisation processes—debordering and rebordering—that participate in the formation of cross-border metropolises. Based on an approach to the border as a social and political construction, we then suggest a conceptual framework that allows for a comprehensive analysis of the changing role and significance of boundaries in the making of cross-border metropolises. Finally, we offer two contrasting empirical case studies, one from the US–Mexico border, the other from a European border. By studying bordering dynamics in San Diego–Tijuana and Geneva, we are able to draw some conclusions about the mechanisms that govern the emergence of cross-border metropolises.

Debordering and the Emergence of Transborder Urban Spaces

Over the last three decades, technological advances in the transport and telecommunication industry, together with the end of the Cold War, the explosion of global markets, the subsequent demise of the Iron Curtain and the emergence of new supra-national political and economic formations such as the European Union and the North American Free Trade Agreement (NAFTA), all point to a vision of a world with increasingly permeable borders, allowing an ever-broadening range of transnational flows. Such developments—part and parcel of the process of globalisation—have led to the simultaneous emergence of what might be termed deterritorialisation, or debordering, that is, the steady decline in the significance of national territory and borders as key elements for organising social life, economic development and political order. For some proponents of the neoliberal economy, the impact of globalisation on state borders was about the emergence of a deterritorialised and therefore "borderless world."[7] Although globalisation has rendered borders more permeable to capital, commodities, information and even

5. Christophe Sohn, "The Border as a Resource in the Global Urban Space: A Contribution to the Cross-Border Metropolis Hypothesis", *International Journal of Urban and Regional Research* (2013), doi: 10.1111/1468-2427.12071.

6. Xiangming Chen, *As Borders Bend: Transnational Spaces on the Pacific Rim* (Lanham, MD: Rowman & Littlefield, 2005), p. 13.

7. Kenichi Ohmae, *The Borderless World: Power and Strategy in the Interlinked Economy* (London: HarperCollins, 1990).

people in some cases, the notion of a world entirely without borders does not seem likely in the foreseeable future.[8]

However, more germane to this article, the opening of territorial borders has unleashed a new era for understanding and conceptualising the changing condition of international borders and the spaces around them. It is now possible to begin to consider how the functions of contact and exchange might, in the future, strike a balance with the traditional functions of boundaries as barriers. In this new paradigm, borders are conceived as interfaces or bridges capable of fostering economic and social development within transborder regions and cities. Empirical explorations for the opening of borders within cross-boundary conurbations and the transformation of cross-border social spaces have emerged, for example, in the transborder urban spaces along the US–Mexico border[9] and in Europe, especially along the Upper Rhine.[10] For Herzog,[11] the emergence of cross-border work and transnational industrialisation (in particular the upsurge of *maquiladoras*, or border assembly plants) generate interdependent social, economic and environmental relationships that underscore the formation of the cross-border metropolis as a specific product of globalisation.

The cross-border metropolis as a socio-spatial paradigm has been challenged by some scholars. They question whether social and economic entities on either side of a state border can ultimately become part of a unified cross-boundary urban space, as opposed to two separate albeit interconnected entities. Despite the evidence of cross-border connections between Tijuana and San Diego, Alegría rejects the hypothesis of a cross-border metropolis, arguing that there is still not sufficient convergence between the two urban entities.[12] Robust cross-border interactions do not necessarily lead to a reduction in differences between the two sides of a shared border. Indeed, Decoville et al. demonstrate that strong cross-border economic interaction can also be fed by core–periphery settings and contribute to the reinforcement of socio-economic differentials.[13]

Moving beyond these seemingly contradictory perspectives, Sohn has developed a conceptual framework that highlights the different ways in which open borders offer opportunities to cross-border metropolises to reinforce their place in global economic networks, and thus enhance their autonomy as cross-border regional entities.[14] Firstly, the border is a means of delimiting national sovereignty by creating an "inside" and an "outside" role—a comparative advantage that allows individuals or organisations to be in contact with the exterior of a territory while remaining safely inside it. In so doing, the border thus generates a *positional benefit* that can result either in a role as territorial gateway, or in the delocalisation

8. Henry Wai-Chung Yeung, "Capital, State and Space: Contesting the Borderless World", *Transactions of the Institute of British Geographers*, Vol. 23, No. 3 (1998), pp. 291–309.

9. Herzog, *Where North Meets South, op. cit.*; Daniel Arreola and William Curtis, *The Mexican Border Cities* (Tucson, AZ: University of Arizona Press, 1993).

10. Remigio Ratti and Shalom Reichman, *Theory and Practice of Transborder Cooperation* (Basel: Helbing & Lichtenhahn, 1993).

11. Herzog, "Cross-National Urban Structure", *op. cit.*

12. Tito Alegría, *Metrópolis Transfronteriza: Revisión de La Hipótesis y Evidencias de Tijuana, México y San Diego, Estados Unidos* (Tijuana: Colegio de la Frontera Norte, 2009).

13. Antoine Decoville, Frédéric Durand, Christophe Sohn and Olivier Walther, "Comparing Cross-Border Metropolitan Integration in Europe: Towards a Functional Typology", *Journal of Borderlands Studies*, Vol. 28, No. 2 (2013), pp. 221–237.

14. Sohn, *op. cit.*

of certain activities to the other side of the border generating a so-called "hinterlandisation." Secondly, a border becomes an asset when it promotes the exploitation of cost differentials. For cross-border metropolises, such a *differential benefit* is reflected in particular by transnational industrialisation (e.g. the *maquiladoras*) and the development of cross-border work. Thirdly, the border area allows *hybridisation* by confronting differences and overcoming constraints through socio-cultural or institutional innovation. Finally, a border can become a symbolic resource as an *object of recognition* that authorises the staging of the international character of the metropolis and/or the political recognition of peripheral actors.

Rebordering and the Challenge for Global Security

One must recognise that globalisation has also produced a trend that runs counter to deterritorialisation and debordering; we call this trend rebordering. It is possible to argue that rebordering and debordering are intrinsically complementary.[15] The opening of state borders goes hand in hand with the emergence of new territorialities at infra- as well as supra-national scales. In many regions, reterritorialisation is on the political agenda and new borders are claimed as a response to globalisation and what is sometimes perceived as a loss of cultural as well as identity markers. The de-activation of certain control and filtering measures is thus accompanied by restructuring of bordering practices in other places, on other levels and by different means.[16] In Europe, and to a lesser extent in North America, the loosening of state borders and the subsequent boom in cross-border interactions has encouraged many border cities and regions to engage in active cross-border cooperation, contributing to a rescaling of territorial governance. The formation of cross-border regions, and particularly those equipped with metropolitan functions, can thus be seen as a reterritorialisation of state borders at the cross-border regional scale.

The second perspective on rebordering deals with the securitisation of state borders. Although the potential security threats that borders represent were already a policy concern before 11 September 2001, it has become a defining paradigm for many governments since the terrorist attacks. As a matter of fact, this ideology has had a major impact on the reclosing of territorial borders, particularly along the US frontier[17] and the external borders of the EU.[18] In the name of the "global war on terror," a sharp increase of controls (at the borders and potentially everywhere) has unfolded, along with the implementation of networked systems of surveillance as well as, in some cases, the erection of walls and security fences. National borders are seen as a line of defence against various threats. Beyond the issue of terrorism, the securitisation discourse also serves to control immigration and reduce the number of migrants from the South entering the North, mainly for economic reasons.[19] Unlike

15. David Newman, "The Lines that Continue to Separate Us: Borders in Our 'Borderless' World", *Progress in Human Geography*, Vol. 30, No. 2 (2006), pp. 143–161.

16. Etienne Balibar, "The Borders of Europe", *Cultural Politics*, Vol. 14 (1998), pp. 216–232.

17. Peter Andreas and Thomas J. Biersteker, *The Rebordering of North America: Integration and Exclusion in a New Security Context* (New York and London: Routledge, 2003).

18. Henk Van Houtum and Roos Pijpers, "The European Union as a Gated Community: The Two-Faced Border and Immigration Regime of the EU", *Antipode*, Vol. 39, No. 2 (2007), pp. 291–309.

19. David Newman, "Contemporary Research Agendas in Border Studies: An Overview", in D. Wastl-Walter (ed.), *The Ashgate Research Companion to Border Studies* (Farnham: Ashgate Publishing, 2011), pp. 33–47.

the first perspective on rebordering, which highlights territorial actors other than the nation-states, this form of rebordering is all about the nation-states. But this process is not only about reclosing borders and retreating back to the nineteenth century. Rather, what is at stake are new forms of filtering/screening of transnational flows, not to stop the movement of people or goods, but to prevent other unwanted elements from entering.[20] This selective porosity is meant to protect territorial-bounded nation-states from undesirable global flows.[21] Balancing economic flows against security imperatives is particularly fragile for the case of the cross-border metropolises, since these two objectives come together and even collide in highly urbanised border zones. On the one hand, cross-border metropolises are places of transnational political, economic and cultural integration. On the other, they are also magnets for immigration, organised crime and other perceived border threats, and therefore hot spots for border securitisation.

In order to disentangle these complex and contradictory dynamics, it is necessary to go beyond the normative views of borders promoted by state actors and accept the idea that it may be possible to couple securitised nationalism and free market transnationalism.[22] In other words, we cannot take borders at "face value."[23] Instead, we need to consider the multifaceted impact of borders on the cross-border metropolitan fabric. Borders are no longer passive lines, but active forces and processes impacting a wide array of domestic and international concerns.[24] The process of bordering is no longer an exclusive prerogative of the state, but involves a wide range of actors whose interests and meanings need to be considered. In short, the cross-border dynamics of globalisation impact the cross-border metropolises while at the same time being shaped by the people, communities, organisations and other forces that define these urban spaces.

The Border Multiple: A Conceptual Framework

Our argument here is that borders must now be viewed in a dynamic way rather than a static one. Our frame of analysis is one of *bordering*. Bordering is, in the end, a socio-political, cultural and economic process; borders have become social constructions, and thus call for shifting emphasis on the everyday bordering and ordering practices that contribute to their (re)production.[25] Following O'Dowd,[26] we also believe that such a dynamic understanding of borders should not neglect their structuring effects. Despite the changes imposed on international boundaries, one must also acknowledge the remarkable resilience of national borders. Borders are "dynamic institutions" where functions inherited from state

20. Gabriel Popescu, *Bordering and Ordering the Twenty-First Century: Understanding Borders* (Lanham, MD: Rowman & Littlefield, 2011).

21. Heather Nicol, "Resiliency or Change? The Contemporary Canada–US Border", *Geopolitics*, Vol. 10, No. 4 (2005), pp. 767–790.

22. Matthew B. Sparke, "A Neoliberal Nexus: Economy, Security and the Biopolitics of Citizenship on the Border", *Political Geography*, Vol. 25, No. 2 (2006), p. 153.

23. Nicol, *op. cit.*

24. Alexander C. Diener and Joshua Hagen, "Theorizing Borders in a 'Borderless World': Globalization, Territory and Identity", *Geography Compass*, Vol. 3, No. 3 (2009), pp. 1196–1216.

25. Henk Van Houtum and Ton Van Naerssen, "Bordering, Ordering and Othering", *Tijdschrift voor economische en sociale geografie*, Vol. 93, No. 2 (2002), pp. 125–136.

26. Liam O'Dowd, "From a 'Borderless World' to a World of Borders: Bringing History Back In", *Environment and Planning D: Society and Space*, Vol. 28, No. 6 (2010), pp. 1031–1050.

Table 1. The Significance of the Border: A Conceptual Framework.

	Structuring effects over agency	
Border dynamics	Constraining	Enabling
Debordering	*Threat*	*Resource*
Rebordering	*Obstacle*	*Shield*

Note: This conceptual framework has been developed by the author in the framework of the EUBORDERSCAPES project. For more details, see <http://www.euborderscapes.eu/>.

institutions are contested and reinterpreted through daily activities.[27] As such, the meaning attached to borders and bordering practices is highly contextual and emerges from contested and contradictory narratives held at different levels of social action (from the local to the national to the supranational).

Inspired by the structuration theory, one way to conceptualise the dialectical condition of borders is to consider the structuring effects of borders "as both medium and outcome of the practices they recursively organize."[28] Actors, by their actions, constantly produce and reproduce structures that both constrain and enable them. Considering the bordering dynamics (debordering and rebordering) in the light of their structuring effects (constraining and enabling) allows us to define four modalities that define borders, and the ways they are interpreted by local and regional actors (Table 1). Instead of associating debordering with opportunities and rebordering with constraints, our framework allows us to consider the significance of borders in a more comprehensive way, taking into account the new global realities that define international borders and the great variety of actors participating in their production. The four modalities should thus be seen as analytical categories whose relevance remains contingent on specific contexts.

When debordering is seen as enabling, the border is considered as a potential *resource* and can be mobilised by actors either to develop an economic benefit (based on value capture) or to promote cross-border reterritorialisation.[29] This way of understanding the role and meaning of borders, we contend, is useful for explaining the formation of cross-border metropolises from both an economic and political point of view. On the other hand, when debordering is seen as a constraint as in the post-9/11 era, the border appears as a *threat* to national security, cohesive identity or economic welfare. There is a sense of insecurity/vulnerability due to cross-border flows of people, goods or services that can lead to increased controls and closing of the borders. When rebordering is seen as an opportunity, the border can play the role of a *shield* that is supposed to protect one's own cultural legacy and economic well-being.[30] In the last instance, where debordering is seen as a constraint, borders are representing *obstacles* to those who wish to develop cross-border connections, whether in the form of trade and economic development, political cooperation or socio-cultural activities.

In the remainder of this article, we explore two empirical cases in which some of these analytical categories surface. The underlying hypothesis is that, as

27. Newman, "The Lines that Continue to Separate Us", *op. cit.*

28. Anthony Giddens, *The Constitution of Society: Outline of the Theory of Structuration* (Cambridge: Polity Press, 1984), p. 25.

29. Sohn, *op. cit.*

30. Van Houtum and Van Naerssen, *op. cit.*

cross-border metropolises evolve in different settings, the trade-offs between the dynamics of globalisation on the one hand and the presence of state borders on the other produce different outcomes. Our goal is to view those outcomes within the theoretical framework articulated above.

Empirical Evidence, Case 1: The San Diego–Tijuana/US–Mexico Border

An important example of the new transfrontier metropolis is found along the border between Mexico and the United States. More than 10 million people today live in transfrontier metropolitan regions that blanket the 2,000-mile boundary from Matamoros–Brownsville in the east to Tijuana–San Diego at the western terminus. Along the California–Mexico border, some 30 million vehicles and nearly 75 million people cross between California and Mexico each year. Urban neighbours are thrust into a complex transnational space of life, work and global security. This massive space of flows can be disaggregated into at least five major transfrontier activity circuits that connect US and Mexican economy and society within a cross-boundary region. Transfrontier labour markets define the spaces within which an estimated 300,000 workers legally travel across the border, from the Mexican to the US side of a transfrontier metropolis, to work in the United States on a daily or weekly basis.[31] Over 60 billion dollars in trade occurs annually across the California–Mexico border, creating giant transfrontier consumer markets.[32] Consumers constitute the most active group of legal border crossers, and are perhaps the primary population that ties together the two sides of the Mexico–US transfrontier metropolis. The North American Free Trade Agreement (NAFTA), with its emphasis on opening borders and increasing economic integration, heightened the transfrontier connections between Mexican and Californian border cities. As a subset of the transborder economy, transnational tourism and related services represent a critical local economic sector, with a long history of connecting US consumers with Mexican vendors. Border tourism is a potentially large source of revenue in the border region, although it is compromised by the uncertainties of security, drug smuggling and border violence. Transfrontier manufacturing is the fourth activity that defines the US–Mexico transborder metropolis. A cheap labour enclave on the Mexican side of the border (i.e. *maquiladoras*) is linked to a headquarter office and warehouse on the US side of the border, creating within the larger fabric of the transfrontier metropolis a "twin plant" system of US investors/managers and Mexican assemblers.[33] Finally, one can argue that transnational housing and land markets represent the last cross-border economic sphere. Landownership is not restricted by national origin on the US side of the border, and is only partially restricted on the Mexican side.[34]

31. See Lawrence Herzog, "Border Commuter Workers and Transfrontier Metropolitan Structure along the United States–Mexico Border", *Journal of Borderlands Studies*, Vol. 5, No. 2 (1990), pp. 1–20.

32. See, for example, Lawrence A. Herzog, *Global Crossroads: Planning and Infrastructure for the California–Baja California Border Region* (San Diego, CA: Transborder Institute, 2009).

33. See Leslie Sklair, *Assembling for Development: The Maquila Industry in Mexico and the United States* (Boston, MA: Unwin Hyman, 1989).

34. In Mexico, foreigners can lease land for a period of time through the *fideicomso* or trust arrangement; this is, in fact, how many Americans came to own land along the Baja California coast south of Tijuana during the boom years of the 1990s and prior to 9/11.

The Era of Debordering (as Resource) in San Diego–Tijuana, 1970–2001

Even before 1970, there was evidence that local interests were prepared to see the border as a resource for the future. As early as the 1960s, the City of San Diego recognised that its future would need to be cast with an eye towards its southern neighbour; a "Border Area Plan" was commissioned in 1965, the first attempt to rethink the growth of San Diego's south bay area and its links with Mexico. That plan forecast San Ysidro as the anchor of the south bay/Mexico connection for the region.[35] In 1973, the City of San Diego commissioned two city planning specialists to carry out a major design and planning study of the future of the region. The resulting landmark report urged the city to rethink its planning strategies, placing greater emphasis on land use, environmental and design approaches that embraced the cross-border connections. As the report stated:

> San Diego thinks of itself as a border town, but in reality it is part of the functioning metropolitan region of San Diego/Tijuana ... San Diego/Tijuana could be the centre of a large international region, a vital meeting point of two living cultures. The metropolis would share its water, its energy, its landscape, its culture, its economy. The border would be converted into a zone of confluence.[36]

By the mid-1970s the burgeoning economic and social ties between San Diego and Tijuana were bringing the cities into closer contact. In 1976, a coalition of US and Mexican institutions sponsored a bicentennial conference series called the "Fronteras Project" which brought together public and private officials from both sides of the border to describe the emerging interrelations of the San Diego–Tijuana region.[37] The following year, construction began on a 60 million dollar light rail connection between downtown San Diego and the Mexican border. One important rationale for building the "border trolley" was the growing interdependence between the two border cities.[38] The trolley's "Blue Line" to the Mexican border opened in 1981, and, at its peak, is used by about 58,000 riders daily. A landmark 1978 study of the California border economy became the state of the art reference tool on the major economic sectors and policy issues for the region over the next decade.[39] At the local level, the San Diego Chamber of Commerce initiated new studies of the Mexican connection.[40] Meanwhile, concern for the growing impact of undocumented Mexican immigrants on the region unleashed a tide of new studies and reports.[41]

---

35. City of San Diego, *San Diego Border Area Plan* (San Diego, 1965).

36. Kevin Lynch and Donald Appleyard, "Temporary Paradise? A Look at the Special Landscape of the San Diego Region", report to the City of San Diego, 1974.

37. See Fronteras, *A View of the Border from Mexico: Proceedings of a Conference* (San Diego, 1976); Fronteras, *San Diego–Tijuana: The International Border in Community Relations: Gateway or Barrier?* (San Diego, 1976).

38. See Metropolitan Transit Development Board, *San Diego-Tijuana: One Region* (San Diego, 1977).

39. State of California and US Economic Development Administration, *Economic Problems of the California Border Region* (Washington, DC, 1978).

40. Economic Research Bureau, Chamber of Commerce, "The Baja California–San Diego County Linkage", in *San Diego Economic Profile* (San Diego, 1978).

41. See, for example, Community Research Associates, *Undocumented Immigrants: Their Impact on the County of San Diego* (San Diego, 1980).

All of these initiatives reflected the larger reality of growing physical connections between San Diego's south bay region and Tijuana. During the 1970s, Tijuana had fully channelised the Tia Juana River, while San Diego responded with a more modest dissipater facility. East of the San Ysidro port of entry, the two cities were negotiating a second border crossing, deemed crucial in light of the growing congestion at the existing border gate.[42] By the early to mid-1980s, the idea of transfrontier cooperation and binational planning began to emerge at local conferences, government meetings, public forums and in the print media.[43] Both the City of San Diego and County of San Diego created special offices to address border issues—the Binational Planning Office in the city; the Department of Transborder Affairs in the county. The economic boom in southern California during the 1980s increased the attention of the national and local media on illegal immigration, while smuggling of narcotics began to increase along the California border. Furthermore, the problems of the border environment began to seriously confront regional planners, most notably those in the realm of border sewage spills, flooding and air pollution.[44]

The early 1990s brought the passage of the NAFTA. Locally, non-governmental and policy organisations began to seriously study the cross-border flows.[45] For the 1996 Republican National Convention held in San Diego, a border briefing book was produced.[46] Meanwhile, concern with physical and land use planning around the question of a second border crossing and a binational airport on the Otay Mesa/Mesa de Otay evolved, along with growing attention to the environmental impacts of cross-border economic development.[47] During the early 1990s, tight budgets wiped out the two local border planning offices at the city and county levels. However, the City of San Diego continued to address cross-border issues through the City Manager Office's Binational Planning Program.[48] The County of San Diego held US–Mexico border summits that brought together county officials and Mexican officials. The county was heavily involved in cooperation with Mexico on service issues ranging from criminal justice, agriculture, environmental health and child services to air pollution and hazardous materials. The San Diego Association of Governments (SANDAG) actively embraced cross-border planning with Tijuana, especially in the areas of watershed research, energy, transportation planning, data collection and the environment.[49]

---

42. The key policy analysis on this issue was: Comprehensive Planning Organization, *International Border Crossing: Otay Mesa/Mesa de Otay* (San Diego, 1978).

43. See, for example, Lawrence A. Herzog, *Planning the International Border Metropolis* (La Jolla, CA: Center for U.S.–Mexican Studies, 1986).

44. See Herzog, *Where North Meets South, op. cit.*, chapter 7, pp. 189–246.

45. See San Diego Dialogue, *Who Crosses the Border* (San Diego, 1994); *Demographic Atlas: San Diego/Tijuana* (San Diego, 1995); *Planning for Prosperity in the San Diego/Baja California Region* (San Diego, 1993).

46. San Diego Dialogue, *The San Diego-Tijuana Binational Region, 1996: A Briefing Book* (San Diego, 1996).

47. See Mark J. Spalding (ed.), *Sustainable Development in San Diego-Tijuana* (La Jolla, CA: Center for U.S.–Mexican Studies, 1999).

48. See Greater San Diego Chamber of Commerce and San Diego Dialogue, *Planning for Prosperity in the San Diego/Baja California Region* (San Diego, 1993).

49. See the SANDAG webpage for the Borders Program, at: <http://www.sandag.org/index.asp?classid=19&fuseaction=home.classhome> (accessed 24 July 2013).

Table 2. US–Mexico Border Region Infrastructure Projects: San Diego–Tijuana 1970–2001 (Planned, Completed, Under Discussion or Phased Out).

Category	Project	Lead actor(s)
Transport	Twin ports/airport	City of San Diego
	Port of entry–Otay Mesa	County of San Diego, California Department of Transportation (CALTRANS), General Service Admin.
	San Diego Eastern Desert Rail Line	Metropolitan Transit Development Bd. (MTDB, now called MTS)
	Virginia Ave. border crossing	US, Mexico federal govt.
	San Ysidro Intermodal Transport Facility	San Diego Association of Governments (SANDAG), CALTRANS, City of San Diego, MTS
	Freeway Rts. 905, 125	CALTRANS
	Widening Otay Mesa Rd.	City of San Diego
	Tijuana light rail transit	Municipality of Tijuana (not completed)
	Tijuana 2000, peripheral highway ring	Secretary of Human Settlements, State of Baja California (SAHOPE)
	International Ave.: circulation plan for border crossing	Municipality of Tijuana
	Road improvements	Municipality of Tijuana
Land use	Las Americas, mixed use development	Land Grant Development (private) w. City of San Diego
	Tijuana pedestrian space redevelopment at border crossing	Municipality of Tijuana
Environment	Wastewater treatment plant	National Development Bank (NADB)/ Border Environmental Cooperation Commission (BECC)
	Ecopark expansion	NADB
	Southbay border wastewater treatment plant, SD	City of San Diego
	Border power plant	Pacific Gas & Electric (private)

An empirical examination of border region infrastructure projects from the period of heightened debordering (1970–2001) is presented in Table 2, which lists projects by category (transport, land use, environment), region, project type and lead actors.[50] Several observations can be made about this period of debordering. First, the lead actors range from local, state and national political jurisdictions to private companies, quasi-public economic development agencies, non-governmental organisations (NGOs) and cross-border coalitions. Second, transportation and environmental projects dominated the landscape during this era. Roads, airports and rail lines were seen as positive assets to accompany cross-border economic development in the era of NAFTA. Environmental projects addressed longer-term resource management policy, and were also driven by NAFTA's emphasis on the environment, through one of two side agreements.

50. These data were gathered over a two-month period from first-hand interviews, public documents, websites and library archival sources. It does not represent a comprehensive list of all border region projects from the period, but rather an approximation of the scope of projects in the planning stages, under construction or completed by the end of this period, the year 2001.

Rebordering (as Obstacle) in San Diego–Tijuana, 2001–2011

During the decade following the 9/11 tragedy in the United States, the San Diego–Tijuana region experienced a powerful phase of rebordering, where protecting the boundary became an obstacle to cross-border social and economic integration. No region in North America was more impacted by the events of 11 September 2001 than the US–Mexico border region. Prior to the World Trade Centre tragedy, the buzzwords of the US–Mexico border were "global market." The California border region was in a boom mode in the 1990s, building on the growing NAFTA-driven economic connections with Mexico. Along its most urbanised sector—the San Diego/Baja border—government and private interests were teaming up to launch a set of ambitious construction projects aimed at creating stronger cross-border ties to Baja California. As mentioned above, transborder highways, rail systems and even airports were on tap for the new millennium. State and local planning agencies were altering their master plans to support building infrastructure needed to assure the huge foreign trade revenues forecast for the region.[51]

Much of this optimism was stopped in its tracks after the events of 11 September 2001. Instead of new highways and border gates, a "wall" of heightened security wedged itself between California and Mexico. The formation of the Department of Homeland Security (DHS) as a cabinet-level agency, consolidating the efforts of immigration, customs, border inspection, transportation security, border patrol and maritime security, marked a watershed moment in 2001–2002. It signalled the emergence of "security" as the primary objective in the management and organisation of the border zone, and the myriad facilities within its jurisdiction.[52]

DHS eventually took the bold move of merging security policy with the needs of regional border users. For example, it developed a way to sort out low-risk border crossers who could be systematically identified and quickly moved across the border. The Secure Entry National Tracking and Information (SENTRI) program has achieved good results, although it needs to be expanded, both for cars and for pedestrians.[53] In addition to the pre-screening of low-risk users, DHS has put a great deal of effort into innovative new tracking technologies, including one for individual border crossers and one for trade goods.[54]

While DHS acknowledged the role of infrastructure and the use of technology in making border crossings more efficient, its primary impact on the border was to introduce "national security" as the operating federal policy "paradigm" for the

---

51. For a description of some of these projects, see Lawrence A. Herzog, "Urban Development Alternatives for the San Ysidro Border Zone", Forum Fronterizo Paper, San Diego Dialogue, 2000.

52. DHS oversees some 22 different agencies divided among four areas of concern: border and transport security, science and technology, information analysis and infrastructure protection, and emergency preparedness. Its objectives are to manage the nation's borders and ports of entry, prevent the unlawful entry of illegal persons or goods, and work overseas to detect and block illegal smuggling operations.

53. Former INS Commissioner Doris Meissner told southern Californians in a December 2002 speech that it is wasteful to create giant traffic jams at the border, when 90 per cent of those being inspected are regular crossers who should not have to be kept waiting in line. If high-risk crossers could be separated from low-risk ones, the overall flow of people and vehicles over the line would be immensely improved and all would benefit. See Kenn Morris, "Moving toward Smart Borders", Forum Fronterizo Paper, San Diego, June 2003.

54. For individuals, DHS created the Border Release Advanced Screening and Selectivity (BRASS) program, which tracks the entry and exit of people into the US. For commerce, it created a program called Fast and Secure Trade (FAST), which screens and tracks goods entering and leaving the US.

US–Mexico border. In fact, it is estimated that from 2001 to 2011, some 100 billion dollars was spent installing the security apparatus along the entire US–Mexico border. This has produced, among other things, some 700 miles of walls, fences and barriers, as well as hidden or mounted surveillance cameras, Predator drones, implanted sensors and more than 20,000 agents guarding the boundary. Some sources claim there are now even "off road forward operating bases," high tech, rudimentary camps in rural areas where DHS agents gather and store intelligence. These kinds of outposts were commonplace during the US wars in Iraq and Afghanistan, where they were meant to house US soldiers deployed in remote areas.[55]

This new border landscape stands in marked contrast to the scenario of the previous decade of the 1990s, where "economic development" had become the overarching theme in US–Mexico relations and the border. On many levels, the formation of a cabinet-level security agency like DHS represents the quintessential example of rebordering as an obstacle along the US–Mexico boundary. It illustrates the use of federal policy to promote the international boundary as a line of demarcation and control, one that does not merely shield and protect the border, but, in effect, impinges on the social space around it, to the detriment of economic actors in particular.[56]

One micro-level example of rebordering as an obstacle during this era lies in the way DHS policy makers handled a local bicycle lane at the San Ysidro, California crossing. In the spring of 2002, DHS closed the bicycle lane, which had been adopted as a sustainable and local community response to the daily post-9/11 logjam of vehicles and pedestrians at the port of entry. The bicycle lane was providing a useful means for local commuters to avoid automobile traffic in the post-9/11 moment. DHS claimed the bicycle lane was dangerous. Critics argued that the federal agencies had undertaken no studies to look for alternatives that would allow an autonomous bike lane to exist.[57] The bicycle lane was eventually restored by the Immigration and Naturalization Service (INS), but it was moved inside the US customs building, thus occupying space used by pedestrians. In 2006, the special bicycle lane was eliminated entirely, and cyclists now have to wait in very long lines with pedestrians, thus compromising their willingness to travel in this manner.[58]

---

55. See Todd Miller, "Immigration Reform=Surveillance Reform", Naked Capitalism, 12 July 2013, available: <http://www.nakedcapitalism.com/2013/07/immigration-reform-surveillance-reform-as-military-tactics-move-inland-from-us-borders.html>, accessed 25 July 2013.

56. During this period, the only transportation projects in play were the planning for a San Ysidro Intermodal Transit Center, including a new southbound pedestrian crossing moved to the east side of the interstate freeway, a proposed Virginia Ave Intermodal Transit Center, a proposed Otay Mesa East third border crossing facility, a proposed San Diego Freight Rail Yard Improvement project, and a proposed South Bay Rapid Transit project. All of the projects remain in the proposal stages. The San Ysidro Intermodal Transit Center is an outgrowth of the proposed remodelling of the San Ysidro border crossing a decade earlier.

57. "Why close out the only option without an alternative?" Rep. Bob Filner (D-San Diego) told the press, "The INS is like a bunch of Keystone Kops. They have no idea of what they are doing, and no notion of what the community wants." See Lawrence Herzog, "The Border: Homeland Security is Not Enough", *San Diego Union Tribune* (op. ed.), Dialog, 26 April 2009, p. F-4.

58. The government claimed it was closing the bicycle lane because people were renting run-down bikes at the border for a few minutes, just to save time. See "US Wants to Close Popular Pedestrian Border Crossing", New York Times.com, 26 August 2007, available: <http://www.nytimes.com/2007/08/26/us/26crossing.html?_r=0>.

Other examples of DHS domination of the San Diego–Tijuana border region infrastructure include the so-called DHS "Border Fence Project" planned for some five miles of the boundary in San Diego. The fence offers another example of the conflict between border security and economic/social well-being. The plan is to construct the most severe of several design options, a version that would insert a militarised zone in a preserved ecological sanctuary. A triple fence would be heavily lit at night with an invasive, oversized paved road running through the centre. It would create a federal security corridor, patrolled by jeeps, vans and other heavy vehicles, in the heart of rare marshlands and sand dunes, and near the gathering places of some of North America's most diverse wildlife, particularly migratory birds. This project was rejected by the State of California's Coastal Commission because it would "do more harm than is necessary to the environment."[59]

More recently the 2013 US immigration bill, named the "Border Security, Economic Opportunity and Immigration Modernization Act" of 2013, while originally intended to address the undocumented status of some 12 million Mexican immigrants in the US, has taken on a profound border security theme. Since the summer of 2013, advocates—mainly from the Republican party in Congress—have been pushing for a so-called "Comprehensive Southern Border Security Strategy." It would add over 20,000 new border patrol officers along the border (doubling the total number to about 40,000), as well as calling for the construction of another 700 miles of border fencing.[60] Nearly 50 billion dollars would be allocated for the building of fences, additional border patrol officers, helicopters, sensors and drones to guard and fortify the international border with Mexico. This new policy direction has been termed a "border surge," and some see it as bringing a militarised, war mentality to the US–Mexico border.[61]

Towards a Post-2011 Balancing Act: Debordering and Rebordering along the California–Mexico Border

It is clear that border policy in San Diego–Tijuana shifted from one extreme in the period 1970–2001 (debordering as resource) to another from 2001–2011 (rebordering as obstacle). Ostensibly, a healthier policy for globalising cross-border metropolises like San Diego–Tijuana would be to seek a balance between the opportunities presented by NAFTA, cross-border trade, labour markets and other activities which clearly bring the two cities and their economies into a common sphere, while at the same time preserving the necessary security a sovereign nation requires in an era of global crime, terrorist acts and other threats to nations. While DHS and other federal agencies spent the decade from 2001 to 2011 building security infrastructure that mostly became more of an obstacle than a more gentle "shield" (to use our conceptualisation of rebordering), cross-border opportunities for San Diego–Tijuana economic development (debordering as a positive resource mechanism) were mostly ignored in the fervour to make the border secure from terrorism. In the future, there are several critical

59. See Terry Rodgers, "Border Battle Brews", *San Diego Union Tribune*, 7 October 2003, pp. B-1–2.

60. See a working version of this bill at: <http://www.schumer.senate.gov/forms/immigration.pdf> (accessed 25 July 2013).

61. Miller, *op. cit.*

debordering projects that could have significant impacts on the long-term economic development of the region, and thus cement the connection in the San Diego–Tijuana cross-border metropolis.

First, to be competitive in the global economy, a region like San Diego–Tijuana needs global transport infrastructure, including a port. Currently, the region is overshadowed by the ports of LA and Long Beach. The port of Ensenada is not considered large enough to serve as a global trade facility.[62] The development of a mega-port facility at Punta Colonet could dramatically reshape the role of Baja ports in California–Mexico trade, and in the entire geography of the region's cross-border flows. A planned mega-port facility at Punta Colonet (80 miles south of Ensenada) would be one of Mexico's largest public infrastructure projects ever built. The port's primary function would be to move imported goods to the interior of the United States. Punta Colonet's impact would be greatly enhanced by a planned rail connection that could easily enter into the US rail system, either through Tecate or Mexicali.

A second form of debordering for the next few decades involves using the port and rail infrastructure to link up with key innovation centres that could be built south of the border. One is an industrial zone along the Tijuana–Tecate corridor, which might eventually produce what has been called a "jobs train," a rail system that could move inputs and outputs from the sub-region to major cities and ports on both sides of the border. A direct rail connection to a major industrial corridor in the eastern Tijuana/Tecate zone would enhance industrial growth, including the Toyota Tacoma factory which currently builds 170,000 truck beds and 20,000 full trucks per year. A second proposed innovation centre would connect with what is being called the "Silicon Border" project, a 10,000-acre science park, with US and Mexican private sector support. The idea is to build one of the premier computer chip (semi-conductor) production zones in the world in the nearby state capital of Baja California–Mexicali.[63] This billion dollar project sees itself as a rival to the current Asian dominance of semi-conductor manufacturing.

Empirical Evidence, Case 2: The Geneva Cross-Border Metropolis

In Europe, the cross-border metropolitan region of Geneva located at the Swiss–French border constitutes a good example to be contrasted with the San Diego–Tijuana case. Although the city of Geneva has only 200,000 inhabitants, the attractiveness of its banking sector and its numerous international as well as non-governmental organisations elevate the city to an important position within the circuits of globalisation. Well anchored within the global space of flows, Geneva's metropolitan development is also closely tied to the mobilisation of the territorial border as a resource, both from a geo-economic and a symbolic point of view. The progressive opening up of the border between Switzerland and France, linked with the EU, has

62. In the long term the Mexican government expects the Port of Ensenada to serve cruise ships and yachting, when it builds the mega-port at Punta Colonet. See David Greenberg, "Mexican Ports Could Take Traffic from LA", *Los Angeles Business Journal*, 16 August 2004.

63. Interestingly, this project was initiated by US entrepreneurs. The chairman of the project, D.J. Hill, claims that "Asia has not just taken manufacturing, but technology too, and a lot of people recognize that we need to do something about this." See Mary Jordan, "Mexican Officials Promote Silicon Border", *Washington Post*, 11 December 2004, p. E-1, available: <http://www.washingtonpost.com/wp-dyn/articles/A56549-2004Dec10.html>.

been a catalyst for economic and political cross-border integration. The emerging cross-border metropolis of Geneva grew to 918,000 inhabitants by 2010, with more than half a million daily border crossings.[64]

Debordering as a Geo-economic Resource for Geneva

Cross-border functional interactions began to accelerate in the 1960s and 1970s due to the vibrant economic growth experienced by Geneva, especially in the banking sector. This led to a widening of cross-border differentials with neighbouring France, both in jobs and wages. A proliferation of cross-border work trips ensued, cementing the increasing functional interdependence between the Swiss international city and its French periphery. The number of cross-border commuters rose from 5,500 in 1965 to 24,500 in 1974 at the time of the first oil shock. In 2001, just before the entry into force of the Agreement on the Free Movement of Persons between Switzerland and the EU,[65] there were almost 32,000 cross-border workers living in France and working in Geneva. Since then, the opening up of the border has been a catalyst for a surge in cross-border labour flows, with more than 63,000 French workers crossing to Geneva in 2013.[66] One should note that these figures include neither international officials nor Swiss citizens who live in France and work in Geneva (some 9,000 officials and 40,000 Swiss workers, respectively) and therefore underestimate the magnitude of the process of integration. As a matter of fact, the cross-border metropolitan region of Geneva (together with Luxembourg and Basel) now has one of the highest rates of cross-border labour movement in Europe.[67]

This highly asymmetrical functional integration has been reinforced by the uneven urban development that characterises the cross-border urban space. On the one side, the canton of Geneva is strongly constrained by the Federal Law on Spatial Planning of 1979 that requires the Swiss cantons to preserve agricultural land on the basis of quotas. Thus, urban growth has tended to spill over to the French side, mainly in the form of residential construction. This metropolitan sprawl is reinforced by a chronic shortage of housing in Geneva and by lower real estate prices across the border in France. Residential growth in the French borderland (notably Annemasse and the Pays de Gex) underscores the emerging polarised land use pattern in the cross-border Geneva–France region: economic growth and jobs concentrate in Geneva, while residential activities cluster across the border in France. Data for the larger cross-border urban region confirms the trend: 75 per cent of workplaces relocated to Switzerland by 2008, while 65 per cent of new housing was built in France from 2000 to 2010.[68]

64. See Grand Genève webpage at: <http://www.grand-geneve.org/grand-geneve/le-territoire/chiffres-cles>.

65. On 21 June 1999, the European Union and Switzerland signed seven bilateral agreements including the Agreement on the Free Movement of Persons, which came into force on 1 June 2002. The right of free movement is complemented by the mutual recognition of professional qualifications, by the right to buy property and by the coordination of social security systems. The same rules also apply to citizens of European Free Trade Association (EFTA) member states (see <http://www.bfm.admin.ch/bfm/en/home/themen/fza_schweiz-eu-efta.html>).

66. OCSTAT L'Office Cantonal de la Statistique (OCSTAT), 2013, at: <http://www.ge.ch/statistique/domaines/apercu.asp?dom=03_05> (accessed 24 July 2013).

67. Decoville et al., *op. cit.*

68. See Grand Genève webpage at: <http://www.grand-geneve.org/grand-geneve/le-territoire/chiffres-cles>.

The Demise of the State Border as an Obstacle: The Construction of a Cross-Border Territorial Organisation

Until the beginning of the 1990s, the core–periphery relationship between Geneva and its French periphery was not institutionally grounded by specific measures for cross-border cooperation or planning for the future development of the cross-border metropolis. The only notable exception was the financial compensation agreement signed in 1973 by the two countries and the subsequent establishment of the Franco-Genevan Joint Consultative Commission.[69] Since then, two events have raised awareness among Geneva authorities about the potentially divisive nature of the national border and, thus, the need to reconsider Geneva's relationship with its French hinterland. First was the development, in the late 1980s, of technology-intensive business parks on the French side that rely on lower labour costs yet benefit from the proximity to the financial centre of Geneva. These new French business ventures were perceived as a threat by the Swiss cantonal authorities. Second, the awareness of Geneva's frontier setting was also reinforced by the refusal of Swiss citizens to integrate with the European Economic Area in the federal vote of 6 December 1992.[70] To counter its position as a quasi-territorial enclave, and to address the possible threat of isolation vis-à-vis the rest of Europe, the government of Geneva realised it must remain competitive against other global cities. Therefore Geneva (which had actually voted yes on the European economic question by more than 80 per cent) realised that it needed to promote its international image and recast its identity as a "gateway to Europe." In both cases, the border location was recognised as a resource to be mobilised. To this end, Geneva politicians turned to their French local counterparts in order to engage in closer cross-border cooperation. Studies focused on planning for the cross-border region were carried out by the Franco-Genevan Regional Committee set up by the consultative commission created in 1973 and composed of local and regional authorities, as well as representatives of the French state. The concept of "Regio Genevensis" was developed with the objective, for the Geneva border region, to affirm the centrality of the Swiss canton.[71] In 1993, a white paper on urban planning was prepared, followed in 1997 by a charter for the development of the cross-border urban agglomeration including 10 development projects. Most of these projects were aimed at enhancing cross-border functional interactions and promoting the international image of the city.

A new milestone was reached in the early 2000s with the creation of the "Franco-Valdo-Genevan agglomeration project" supported by the French as well as the Swiss governments. While the support from France is mainly symbolic, in the form of recognition of the cross-border project goals, the Swiss Confederation is providing financial support.[72] Developed between 2004 and 2006, the Franco-

69. According to the fiscal compensation agreement, 3.5 per cent of the cross-border payroll is paid by Geneva to the French border towns in proportion to the number of cross-border workers they host. In 2011, the amount refunded to the French towns reached 190 million Euros. See <http://archives.tdg.ch/geneve/actu/fonds-frontaliers-compensation-financiere-genevoise-atteint-records-2011-12-21>.

70. François Moullé, "L'agglomération transfrontalière genevoise: acteurs, stratégies et fonctions internationales", in B. Reitel et al. (eds.), *Villes et frontières* (Paris: Economica, 2002), pp. 114–123.

71. Jean-Pierre Leresche and Michel Bassand, "The Emergence of the 'Lemanique Metropole': A Process of Apprenticeship', *Political Geography*, Vol. 14, No. 4 (1995), pp. 401–417.

72. See Christophe Sohn and Bernard Reitel, "The Role of National States in the Construction of Cross-Border Metropolitan Regions in Europe: A Scalar Approach", *European Urban and Regional Studies* (2013), doi: 10.1177/0969776413512138.

Valdo-Genevan agglomeration project brings together local and regional authorities on either side of the border. Joint planning of transportation infrastructure and urban development highlights the agenda of this cross-border cooperation initiative. Financial support from the Swiss Confederation facilitated the building of the CEVA railway junction between the Cornavin station in Geneva and Annemasse, thus creating a transborder connection between the Swiss and French rail networks. A cross-border light rail line is also planned.

There are still many policy challenges ahead. For example, spatial and socio-economic inequalities continue to characterise the cross-border metropolis. Traffic congestion from cross-border worker flows tends to generate national resentment. An urban development strategy specifically recommends that by 2030 the population growth should be shared equally between Switzerland and France and that a third of the jobs created should be located in France by mean of fiscal incentives to companies.[73] This more equitable sharing of economic activities and residence evokes the idea of development of a common sense of belonging, a shared vision and an imagined future of cross-border cooperation. But it is a long-term goal and stakeholders on both sides of the border are well aware of its respective strengths and weaknesses. Without the establishment of an ad hoc tax and regulatory framework by the French government, the authorities of Annemasse know they are unlikely to attract financial institutions and international organisations into their territorial jurisdiction.

In 2012, the formation of the Geneva cross-border metropolitan region has been pushed a step further with the implementation of a new juridical tool (called "Local Grouping for Cross-border Cooperation") which allows for a more permanent mode of governance and the reinforcement of the autonomy of the cross-border entity vis-à-vis the Franco-Genevan Regional Committee. In the meantime, the leadership of Geneva over the cross-border agglomeration is asserted symbolically through the choice of "Greater Geneva" as a new name.

Debordering as a Threat: The Geneva Fears against Cross-Border Integration

While a majority of the Geneva political and economic elite supports this process of building a cross-border metropolis and sees the border as a resource for the international competitiveness of the city, a xenophobic minority emerged during the 2000s. This group expressed resentment against French cross-border workers. Its base comes mainly from the far right regionalist party named Mouvement des Citoyens Genevois, or MCG (Geneva Citizens' Movement), who blame the cross-border workers for unemployment, violence and insecurity; this group often campaigns for a rebordering of the national territory. Although it is a minority, the MCG still received almost 15 per cent of the votes at the cantonal elections in 2009 (17 representatives out of 100 in the Genevan council); more recently they were big winners in the local elections in 2011.

The main reasons for this xenophobic discourse (which portrays the border as a threat to socio-economic welfare) lies in the tensions in the local labour market resulting from the opening of borders, and the perception of increased competition

73. Christophe Sohn, Bernard Reitel and Olivier Walther, "Cross-Border Metropolitan Integration in Europe: The Case of Luxembourg, Basel, and Geneva", *Environment and Planning C: Government and Policy*, Vol. 27, No. 5 (2009), pp. 922–939.

between Swiss workers and cross-border workers.[74] The relatively high unemployment rate in Geneva, by comparison with the rest of Switzerland (6 per cent in Geneva vs. 3.3 per cent nationally) is fuelling this tension. Cross-border workers account for about a quarter of all jobs in Geneva but the vast majority occupy low-skilled positions in the banking, trade and catering sectors. Most of those jobs would not be taken by local residents, either because of the shortage of labour (for example, nurses at the University Hospitals of Geneva) or due to a lack of interest in strenuous work (such as in restaurants).[75] Despite these economic realities, the cross-border worker is perceived, by some Swiss residents, as "a profiteer who makes a well-paid living in Geneva and spends his money in France."[76]

Conclusions

In this article, we have provided a conceptual framework for the analysis of what we call "bordering dynamics." We contend that this approach exposes various meanings and roles that borders will increasingly play in the context of globalisation and territorial restructuring. Applied to the cases of San Diego–Tijuana and Geneva–French periphery, such an analytical lens allows one to better scrutinise the logics at play and disentangle the contradictory dynamics that shape the cross-border metropolises. Border functions and significance are no longer merely defined by nation-states only, but rather result from the activities and practices of various actors, including local and regional communities, political entrepreneurs, transborder networks or institutions and global economic players. As social and political constructions, international borders themselves become laboratories for revealing the mechanisms that will govern the future organisation of cross-border metropolitan spaces.

The cross-border integration trajectories uncovered for the two case studies explored in this article stand in stark contrast. This is, of course, not entirely surprising given the severe differences between the geo-economic, cultural as well as institutional setting that prevails in North America as opposed to Europe. On the one hand, San Diego–Tijuana was forced to confront a drastic rebordering imposed by the US federal government after 2001, one that has had an enormous negative impact upon cross-border social and economic interactions since then. Conceived as a kind of shield constructed to protect the homeland, the border has morphed into an obstacle to local and regional cross-border businesses. On the other hand, Geneva was able to benefit from a gradual shift towards what we term a debordering condition, one aimed at strengthening cross-border ties with its French counterpart. Although Switzerland is not part of the EU, there is clearly a Europeanisation dynamic at play in the case of Greater Geneva, particularly as far as cross-border territorial governance is concerned.

Despite these obvious contrasts, similarities between the two cross-border metropolises can also be identified. These yield more general conclusions about the logic and the processes that shape these urban configurations that are so emblematic of

74. Jean-Baptiste Delaugerre, "Être frontalier en Suisse: le cas du canton de Genève", in R. Belkacem and I. Pigeron-Piroth (eds.), *Le travail frontalier au sein de la Grande Région Saar-Lor-Lux: pratiques, enjeux et perspectives* (Nancy: Presses universitaires de Nancy, 2012), pp. 237–253.

75. *Ibid.*, pp. 237–253.

76. *Ibid.*, p. 243.

twenty-first-century globalisation. First, it seems clear that opening the frontier allows border cities and urban regions to strengthen their economic development and reinforce their position within the larger networks of globalisation. In both San Diego–Tijuana and Geneva, strong economic differentials have triggered cross-border flows (trade, workers and so forth). These social or economic exchanges in the areas of labour, production networks, shopping or residence have given shape to functionally integrated urban regions that extend across national borders. Cross-border planning and infrastructure development, particularly in the area of transport infrastructure, is also part of the dynamic, although it is highly dependent on the willingness of political actors to cooperate.

Second, it is the convergence of the various actors involved in seeing the border as a resource that ends up being essential for cross-border metropolises to develop. Such a convergence of interests, be it explicit or implicit, does not simply result from the opening up of borders and the rise of new opportunities that such a debordering may represent. This is, indeed, a process that becomes contingent upon negotiations, as well as political struggles, to find the proper balance of power. The way borders are conceived is a contested process by nature since they are political and social constructions that incorporate as well as shape power relations. The cross-border metropolis is therefore an ongoing construction, a contested process where the different meanings of the border are to be (re)negotiated. Such a process is also highly "unstable" as other interests and visions concerning the meanings of borders can rise and challenge the development of the cross-border metropolis. In San Diego–Tijuana it is the US national rebordering that has impacted the development of the metropolis by recasting the border as a shield, in effect turning what was a positive feature into an obstacle to those who wish to cross it. Following a decade of closure and enhanced controls, it appears that a better balance between cross-border economic development and security policy is moving back onto the political agenda. At stake ultimately is the negotiation of the best way to mediate the enabling effect of debordering (the border as a resource) and rebordering (the border as a shield). In the case of Geneva, the debordering process is supported by most of the local political actors as well as the nation-states as the best option for the development of the cross-border region. However, these growing socio-economic interdependencies also generate discontent, especially among the more conservative Swiss residents who see the open border as a threat to their national interests and well-being. Further negotiation and consensus building is needed in order to sustain the cross-border metropolitan integration process.

In the end, what appears to be critical is the capacity of cross-border metropolises to constantly adapt their transfrontier strategy to promote consensus among key players in order to counter the dynamics that represent a hindrance to economic and territorial infrastructure development. When the cross-border metropolis is conceived as a socio-economic entity with some strategic capability, the border should not only be viewed as an economic resource (i.e. a source of revenue), but also as a political asset mobilised through the framework of a "place-making" strategy. This will allow the promotion of a shared spatial imaginary (e.g. a vision of future urban development), the development of governance capacity based on trust and willingness to cooperate, and the building of a common sense of belonging. Taken together, these become the building blocks of an emerging regional resilience that will empower cross-border metropolises to embrace the challenges of globalisation and the different bordering dynamics that may emerge. Both San Diego–Tijuana and Geneva–French periphery will face these challenges in the coming decades.

Policing the Workplace and Rebuilding the State in "America's Finest City": US Immigration Control in the San Diego, California–Mexico Borderlands

JOSEPH NEVINS

In 2008, US immigration authorities raided the French Gourmet restaurant, bakery and catering business in San Diego, California. They arrested 18 employees for working in the United States without authorisation, and ultimately deported most of them. The raid reflects a growing effort by the federal government over time to compel employers to cooperate with state-led efforts to police workplaces and effectively cleanse them of unauthorised workers. This article traces the institutional genealogy of such efforts while demonstrating how they are part and parcel of a general "hardening" of US socio-territorial boundaries and the growth of a state apparatus charged with policing those boundaries. In doing so, the article seeks to illustrate how these developments articulate with the shifting nature of the state—in the contemporary United States and elsewhere—and how it defines and produces matters of security and wellbeing. It is a state that sits uneasily at the intersection of processes of neoliberalism, securitisation and the production of increasing precariousness for workers.

On 15 May 2008, after closing down surrounding streets, a dozen armed US immigration agents stormed the French Gourmet, a well-known, high-end restaurant, bakery and catering business in San Diego, California, a city that abuts the US–Mexico boundary. The agents arrested 18 non-US-citizen employees for working there without the federal government's authorisation, and took away boxes of files and computer hard drives.[1]

Among the factors that were striking about the incident is that it took place during Barack Obama's presidency—not because it represents a difference in substance, but more one of form: the Obama administration's approach to violations of immigrant employment law has been seemingly less public and less violent than that adopted by its predecessor, the administration led by George W. Bush. Bush was far more likely to use high-profile raids of workplaces, such as the one that occurred at Agriprocessors, Inc., the largest kosher slaughterhouse and meatpacking plant in the United States, in Postville, Iowa in May 2008,[2] a raid

1. Sarah Kershaw, "Immigration Crackdown Steps into the Kitchen", *The New York Times*, 7 September 2010, p. D3.

2. Jill Lindsey Harrison and Sarah E. Lloyd, "Illegality at Work: Deportability and the Productive New Era of Immigration Enforcement", *Antipode*, Vol. 44, No. 2 (2012), pp. 365–385; Jens Manuel Krogstad, "Iowa Raid Helps Shape Immigration Debate", *USA Today*, 9 May 2013.

that resulted in the arrest of nearly 400 non-citizen workers. Although the Department of Homeland Security (the federal department responsible for, among other things, immigration policing) under Obama employs workplace raids on occasion,[3] the administration's preferred modus operandi is that of the "silent raid," involving the sending of "no-match" letters to business establishments warning them that workers without proper documentation are in their employ, that the employees' reported social security numbers do not match their names, and that they need to rectify the lack of correspondence.[4] Because mistakes happen, the response might involve, among other steps, an employee or employer correcting a misrecording or misreporting of information. In most cases, however, the letters result in the firing of employees given that, more often than not, a situation of no-match reflects the fact that they do not have the legal right to work in the United States, typically because their very presence in the country is not sanctioned by the federal government. Thus, instead of having to drag workers out of their workplaces, which would likely lead to embarrassing media images and an accompanying outcry from civil libertarians and immigrant advocates, the Obama White House has opted instead for quietly forcing employers to fire unauthorised workers. At the same time, it has pressured many employers to check more assiduously than they have in the past their employees' documents to verify that they have a legal right to work in the United States.[5]

It appears that the French Gourmet raid was a response to what federal authorities perceived as an effective refusal by the establishment's owner and management to cooperate with "silent raids." As explained in a press release of 21 April 2010 from US Immigration and Customs Enforcement, the French Gourmet continued to employ individuals after receiving no-match letters, accepting new documentation from the employees in question despite knowing that the documentation was false.[6] Because of this and related transgressions, Michel Malécot, the French Gourmet's owner, faced the possibility of 30 years in prison, almost $4 million in fines, and the seizure of his restaurant.[7] This perhaps helps to explain why he eventually pleaded guilty to a relatively small charge, a misdemeanour one of ongoing employment of unauthorised workers. One of his managers, Richard Kauffmann, also pleaded guilty to hiring at least 10 "illegal" workers in 2006 and 2007, a felony.[8] In December 2011, a federal judge sentenced

3. *Odessa American* (Texas), "ICE: 38 People Arrested at Construction Site", 17 May 2011; William K. Rashbaum and Mosi Secret, "US Seizes 14 7-Eleven Stores in Immigration Raids", *The New York Times*, 17 June 2013.

4. David Bacon and Bill Ong Hing, "The Rise and Fall of Employer Sanctions", *Fordham Urban Law Journal*, Vol. 38 (2010), pp. 77–105; Julia Preston, "Illegal Workers Swept From Jobs in 'Silent Raids'", *The New York Times*, 9 July 2010, p. A1; Virginia Parks, "Enclaves of Rights: Workplace Enforcement, Union Contracts, and the Uneven Regulatory Geography of Immigration Policy", *Annals of the Association of American Geographers*, Vol. 104, No. 2 (2014), pp. 329–337.

5. Manuel Valdes, "Audits of Companies for Illegal Immigrants Rise", *USA Today*, 23 December 2012.

6. US Immigration and Customs Enforcement, "San Diego-area Bakery, its Owner and Manager, Indicted on Federal Charges for Hiring Undocumented Workers", press release from US Customs and Immigration Enforcement, San Diego, CA, 21 April 2010, available: <http://www.ice.gov/news/releases/1004/100421sandiego.htm>.

7. Kershaw, *op. cit.*

8. Kristina Davis, "French Gourmet Owner Admits Illegal Hiring", *San Diego Union-Tribune*, 13 October 2011.

Malécot to five years of supervised probation; Kauffmann received three years of supervised probation, and the business was fined almost $400,000.[9]

Like the many high-profile immigration raids conducted by the G.W. Bush administration, the Obama administration's action against the French Gourmet was a way of "sending a message" to uncooperative employers. As a Department of Homeland Security (DHS) press statement released on the day of Malécot's and Kauffmann's sentencing stated, their convictions "should remind all employers—including corporations, owners and upper management—that they are equally bound by this country's immigration laws and cannot simply disregard their legal obligations. When employers do not comply, we will take vigorous enforcement action to ensure they do not profit from this illegal tactic."[10] The "reminder" seems to have worked: "If their strategy is to get the attention of the industry," the head of the California Restaurant Association told *The New York Times* in 2010, "mission accomplished."[11]

No doubt, the threat of "vigorous enforcement action" (in addition to recent experience) helps to explain the fact that the French Gourmet now uses E-Verify, an internet-based system run by the US Department of Homeland Security, as the DHS describes it, "that allows businesses to determine the eligibility of their employees to work in the United States."[12] It is the Obama administration's hope that mandatory use of E-Verify will be phased in universally over the next few years. Outside of Arizona and Mississippi, both of which require that all employers—in both the public and private sectors—enrol in the programme (it is also compulsory for federal agencies and contractors), E-Verify is officially a voluntary programme for businesses, although federal authorities often apply pressure on employers, reportedly by sometimes threatening companies with potentially costly audits or investigations of their employees, to adopt it.[13] (At least another 11 states require that public agencies and/or recipients of public contracts use E-Verify.[14]) As of February 2013, 429,100 business locations across the United States were reportedly using E-Verify; 3,634 of them were in San Diego County. Although these numbers only comprise 11 per cent of US employers,[15] it seems that they are disproportionately large ones as they screen more than 20 per cent of all new hires in the United States.[16]

---

9. US Department of Homeland Security (US DHS), "San Diego-Area Bakery Owner, Manager Sentenced for Employing Illegal Workers. Defendants Fined Nearly $400,000, Including $10,000 in Restitution for Injured Employee", 22 December 2011; Dana Littlefield, "Two Get Probation in French Gourmet Case", *San Diego Union-Tribune*, 22 December 2011.

10. US DHS, *op. cit.*

11. Kershaw, *op. cit.*

12. US Citizen and Immigration Services, "E-Verify", available: <http://www.uscis.gov/portal/site/uscis/menuitem.eb1d4c2a3e5b9ac89243c6a7543f6d1a/?vgnextoid=75bce2e261405110VgnVCM1000004718190aRCRD&vgnextchannel=75bce2e261405110VgnVCM1000004718190aRCRD>.

13. See, for example, Lee Romney and Cindy Chang, "Latino Food Chain's Participation in E-Verify Leaves a Bad Taste", *Los Angeles Times*, 17 September 2012.

14. See Marc R. Rosenblum, *E-Verify: Strengths, Weaknesses, and Proposals for Reform* (Washington, DC: Migration Policy Institute, 2011).

15. Elizabeth Aguilera, "Coming: Employment Verification for All", *San Diego Union-Tribune*, 12 February 2013.

16. Rosenblum, *op. cit.* According to the Department of Homeland Security, as of January 2014, more than 500,000 employers use E-Verify. See "Half a Million Companies Now Participate in E-Verify", press release from US Immigration and Citizenship Services, 23 January 2014, available: <http://www.uscis.gov/news/news-releases/half-million-companies-now-participate-e-verify-0>.

Historically and contemporarily, the business community has been generally opposed to measures like E-Verify, one reason being the additional time, paperwork and costs they require. Nonetheless, it seems like many had become resigned to E-Verify's spread by early 2013. As Ruben Barrales, former head of the San Diego Regional Chamber of Commerce, told the *San Diego Union Tribune*, "It's inevitable we are moving in that direction."[17]

Why and how "we are moving in that direction"—one of growing state policing of labour in terms of citizenship and immigration status and a concomitant geographical expansion involving an increase in policing of migrants within the US interior—and what it says about the ever-changing nature of the state in the United States (and beyond) is the focus of this article. In this vein, it first provides a brief overview of the policing of immigrant workers and their employers by the US federal government since the mid-1800s. It then examines the development of the immigration and boundary control apparatus as a way of helping to explain how and why the increase in workplace policing has come about. In conclusion, the article explores what this socio-geographic expansion says about the changing nature of the state, arguing that it reflects and embodies, among other things, decreasing protection of worker rights and wellbeing on the part of the state. The expansion also manifests the growth of a securitised bureaucracy—one that draws upon and produces violence through, among other means, constructing ever-sharper distinctions between insiders and outsiders—and its increasing ability to shape collective ways of seeing and being within the United States.

Illegalising Labouring Bodies—of a Particular Sort

Despite widespread anti-immigrant sentiment as well as violence—much of it labour-based, involving armed conflicts between native-born and immigrant workers in the mid-1800s[18]—the US Congress did not vote on any bills to restrict immigration in the first few decades of the nineteenth century, most likely due to the power of capital and its need for the very immigrants protested by a fragmented nativist movement. Indeed, to the extent that the federal government did take action, it was usually to facilitate immigration.[19] During the Civil War in the mid-nineteenth century, for example, the federal government implemented the Act to Encourage Immigration (1864), the first comprehensive federal immigration law. The legislation established the first US Immigration Bureau, the primary function of which was to increase immigration so that US industries would have a sufficient labour supply during the Civil War. Despite the legislation's repeal in 1868, it laid the foundation for the proliferation of private labour recruitment agencies that were vital in encouraging European emigration in the late nineteenth century.[20]

After the war, during the 1870s and 1880s, industrialists actively recruited immigrant labour. As the immigrant influx began to take on a life of its own, immigration again became a serious handicap for organised labour as employers took

17. Aguilera, *op. cit.*

18. See Kitty Calavita, *US Immigration Law and the Control of Labour: 1820–1924* (London and Orlando, FL: Academic Press Inc., 1984).

19. Much of this section and of the next is taken from Joseph Nevins, *Operation Gatekeeper and Beyond: The War on "Illegals" and the Remaking of the US–Mexico Boundary* (New York: Routledge, 2010).

20. *Ibid.*

advantage of the enlarged labour pool to lower wages and break strikes.[21] This was a time of dramatic industrial expansion, mechanisation of production being an important component of the growth. Mechanisation allowed industrialists to replace skilled, unionised labour with "the thousands of unskilled, nonunionized immigrants that entered the country each month."[22]

The post-Civil War era was one during which organised labour was still able to grow to unprecedented levels—reaching an apex in 1885 and enabling organised labour to engage in highly effective strikes—because of rapid industrialisation (and thus significant growth of the workforce). It was also a time of strong employer efforts to undermine labour organising. Industry's primary weapon against the increasing power of organised labour was, as before, the importation and employment of recent immigrant workers. Yet, despite this strategy of pitting worker against worker, a notion of solidarity towards immigrant labourers of European descent among unions was stronger than the restrictionist tendency for much of the nineteenth century.[23]

Although organised labour often had a somewhat benign attitude towards European immigrants in the nineteenth century, it did not extend such levels of relative solidarity to non-European immigrants. Indeed, there was an overtly nativist and racist component of a significant sector of the labour movement. New waves of immigration and disruptive economic changes brought about by accelerated industrialisation during the US Civil War provided a fertile context for organised labour's nativism.[24] Organised labour, for example, played a major role in obtaining the passage of the Chinese Exclusion Act of 1882.[25]

Prohibiting the immigration of Chinese labourers, the law had an explicitly racist component, but it also had a class-based one as it was intended to protect native-born workers against what was framed as unfair competition from Chinese workers. As historian Erika Lee argues, the law marked "the first time in American history that the United States barred a group of immigrants because of its race and class."[26] Chinese Exclusion also helped give rise to the establishment of policing of migrants along the United States' territorial boundaries.[27]

The conflation of race, class and immigrant exclusion was not limited to the population of Chinese descent. In the context of the Depression of the 1930s, Mexicans also became a convenient scapegoat, one blamed for a variety of social ills, particularly those related to unemployed labour and a shortage of paid work. It was in such a climate that the forced repatriation of tens of thousands of Mexican nationals—and the expulsion to Mexico of large numbers of US citizens of Mexican descent—took place in the 1930s.[28]

---

21. See Gwendolyn Mink, *Old Labour and New Immigrants in American Political Development: Union, Party, and State, 1875–1920* (Ithaca and London: Cornell University Press, 1986).
22. Calavita, *US Immigration Law and the Control of Labour, op. cit.*, pp. 39–40.
23. A.T. Lane, *Solidarity or Survival?—American Labour and European Immigrants, 1830–1924* (London, New York and Westport, CT: Greenwood Press, 1987), p. 211. See also Calavita, *US Immigration Law and the Control of Labour, op. cit.*, pp. 44–66.
24. Mink, *op. cit.*
25. See Erika Lee, *At America's Gate: Chinese Immigration during the Exclusion Era, 1882–1943* (Chapel Hill, NC: University of North Carolina Press, 2003).
26. *Ibid.*, p. 4.
27. *Ibid.*, pp. 151–188.
28. See Francisco E. Balderrama and Raymond Rodríguez, *Decade of Betrayal: Mexican Repatriation in the 1930s* (Albuquerque, NM: University of New Mexico Press, 1995).

Yet, despite such developments, what is striking about the US immigration control regime throughout most of the 1900s was the effective refusal of the state to police immigrants in relation to employment. Instead, the state functioned more as a facilitator of low-wage immigration. Indeed, in response to labour shortages brought about by the Second World War, the US and Mexican governments initiated in 1942 a contract labour programme, the so-called Bracero Program. Over a 22-year period, the programme brought approximately five million Mexican contract (temporary) workers to the United States.[29]

Many expected the Bracero Program to reduce unauthorised immigration from Mexico, but the opposite seems to have happened. Many growers continued to prefer hiring unauthorised migrants as it was less cumbersome and less expensive than hiring braceros. In this regard, grower practices significantly facilitated the rise in extralegal migration. Through its actions, moreover, the US Immigration and Naturalization Service (INS) actually encouraged unsanctioned migration by legalising unauthorised migrants already residing in the United States. This served to increase "illegal" immigration from Mexico as the news spread that the easiest manner to obtain a bracero contract was to enter the United States clandestinely.[30]

An important contributing factor to the continuation and rise in unauthorised migration was the immunity enjoyed by employers of undocumented migrants. Although Congress had passed a law in 1952 that made it illegal to "harbor, transport, or conceal" extralegal entrants, the law considered employment of unauthorised migrants *not* to be a form of harbouring. Congress later even rejected an amendment to the law that would have penalised employers who *knowingly* employed undocumented workers.[31]

That said, as the Border Patrol and the larger apparatus of control grew, so too did the federal government's ability to police immigrants and to challenge the resistance of (unauthorised) migrant labour-dependent employers, especially in the agricultural sector. In this regard, the state's facilitation of labour migration—through the Bracero Program—was coupled with increased disciplining of those sectors of capital resistant to the state's attempt to regulate it. Thus, especially in south Texas in the early 1950s, the state had to exert significant pressure on recalcitrant employers to gain their acceptance of the Bracero Program and the right of the federal government to regulate their non-US-national workers.[32]

It was not until the 1970s that matters relating to the unauthorised employment of non-citizen workers began to change legislatively. In 1971, Representative Peter Rodino (Democrat, New Jersey) began a series of hearings that took place throughout the United States on unauthorised immigration. Out of these hearings (1971–1972) emerged a five-volume Congressional document on the putative dangers of unauthorised immigration and the negative effects of "illegal" immigrants on

29. See Kitty Calavita, *Inside the State: The Bracero Program, Immigration, and the INS* (New York: Routledge, 1992); and Don Mitchell, *Bracero* (Athens, GA: University of Georgia Press, 2012).

30. Calavita, *Inside the State, op. cit.*, pp. 24–25, 28. See also Ernesto Galarza, *Merchants of Labour: The Mexican Bracero Story* (Charlotte, NC and Santa Barbara, CA: McNally & Loftin Publishers, 1964); and Kelly Lytle Hernández, *Migra! A History of the US Border Patrol* (Berkeley, CA: University of California Press, 2010).

31. Calavita, *Inside the State, op. cit.*, pp. 66–70.

32. Lytle Hernández, *op. cit.*

employment and wage rates.[33] In early 1972, a House immigration subcommittee drew up recommendations which the House Judiciary Committee, led by Rodino, endorsed. The resulting legislation served as the basis for much of the congressional debates on issues relating to unauthorised immigration and boundary enforcement during the 1970s and 1980s. At the centre of the proposals was an employer sanctions bill similar to one successfully passed in the California assembly in 1971 that established fines against employers hiring unauthorised workers.[34]

Members of the US House of Representatives, in a political context in which key elements of organised labour ranging from the United Farm Workers to the American Federation of Labor and Congress of Industrial Organizations (AFL-CIO) were calling for heightened policing of unauthorised immigrant labour,[35] introduced a number of employer sanctions bills over the next few years that passed by wide margins. But these bills died in the Senate because of the opposition of Senator James Eastland (Democrat, Mississippi), the chair of the Senate Judiciary Committee, a pro-segregation cotton grower with strong ties to southern agribusiness. Eastland refused to allow hearings to go forth on the Senate's versions of the bills, despite strong support for the legislation from the Nixon and Ford administrations. Eastland's opposition notwithstanding, Ford established a cabinet-level Domestic Council of Illegal Migration in 1975, chaired by his attorney general, that recommended an employer sanctions law and a legalisation programme.[36]

The Carter administration (1977–1980) continued the trend. In the summer of 1977, Carter announced his immigration plan, one that included a call to double the size of the Border Patrol and closely resembled that of Congressman Rodino.[37] In launching the proposal, Carter argued that unauthorised immigrants "had breached the Nation's immigration laws, displaced many American citizens from jobs, and placed an increased financial burden on many state and local governments."[38] His bill included employer sanctions, a legalisation programme and enhanced boundary enforcement, but it was ultimately unsuccessful. It was in the aftermath of this temporary defeat that Carter established his US Select Commission on Immigration and Refugee Policy in October 1978 (also known as the Hesburgh Commission).[39]

---

33. Kitty Calavita, "The New Politics of Immigration: Balanced-Budget Conservatism and the Symbolism of Proposition 187", *Social Problems*, Vol. 43, No. 3 (1996), p. 289.

34. David G. Gutiérrez, *Walls and Mirrors: Mexican Americans, Mexican Immigrants, and the Politics of Ethnicity* (Berkeley, Los Angeles and London: University of California Press, 1995), p. 189; California Assemblyman Dixon Arnett sponsored the legislation. Regarding the legislation's effects, see Jim McVicar, "Law Bans Hiring of Illegal Aliens", *The San Diego Union*, 15 November 1971, p. B-1+; Kitty Calavita, *California's "Employer Sanctions": The Case of the Disappearing Law* (San Diego, CA: Center for US–Mexican Studies, University of California, San Diego, 1982. By mid-1978, 14 states and Puerto Rico had passed similar legislation. See Sasha G. Lewis, *Slave Trade Today: American Exploitation of Illegal Aliens* (Boston, MA: Beacon Press, 1979), p. 168.

35. See Frank Bardacke, *Trampling Out the Vintage: Cesar Chavez and the Two Souls of the United Farm Workers* (New York: Verso, 2011).

36. Kitty Calavita, "US Immigration and Policy Responses: The Limits of Legislation", in Wayne Cornelius et al. (eds.), *Controlling Immigration: A Global Perspective* (Stanford, CA: Stanford University Press, 1994), pp. 65–66.

37. Timothy J. Dunn, *The Militarisation of the US–Mexico Border, 1978–1992: Low-Intensity Conflict Doctrine Comes Home* (Austin, TX: The Center for Mexican American Studies, the University of Texas at Austin, 1996), p. 36; Gutiérrez, *op. cit.*, p. 200.

38. Gutiérrez, *op. cit.*, p. 200.

39. Calavita, "US Immigration and Policy Responses", *op. cit.*, p. 66.

This "blue-ribbon" commission helped to reframe official debate around immigration. Its final report called for a substantial increase in resources for boundary policing and interior enforcement, the passage of legislation making it illegal for employers to hire unauthorised migrants, and the establishment of a programme to legalise unauthorised immigrants residing in the United States. In championing both increased boundary and interior enforcement, however, the Commission acknowledged that existing enforcement efforts were selective given the unequal amount of resources focused on the border region as opposed to interior enforcement, thus serving to create a disproportionate emphasis on unauthorised migrants from Mexico and, to a lesser extent, Central America. But the Commission argued that such an emphasis was necessary and should continue given the difficulty of implementing effective employer sanctions and that it is "both more humane and cost effective to deter people from entering the United States than it is to locate and remove people from the interior."[40] More generally, enhanced boundary enforcement efforts were, according to the Commission, a necessary precondition for the implementation of a legalisation programme, otherwise such a programme "could serve as an inducement for further illegal immigration."[41] Although the Commission only had the power to make recommendations, its recommendations, and the assumptions that informed them, served as the basis for subsequent debate and legislation regarding immigration control. Its final report proved more powerful than it might have given its publication at a time of rising immigration restrictionist sentiment and a growing perception of an immigration and border crisis.

One year after the Select Commission had published its recommendations, the first versions of what would become the 1986 Immigration Reform and Control Act (IRCA) emerged out of the Senate and House judiciary committees, both closely mirroring the Commission's proposals. While the bill (also known as Simpson-Mazzoli after its Senate and House sponsors, respectively) easily passed the Senate, concerns of civil rights advocates, the US Chamber of Commerce and growers effectively defeated it in the House. A number of notable changes over the years, among them a clause that released employers from the responsibility of having to verify the authenticity of their employees' identity documents, led to the bill's passage in October 1986.[42]

IRCA obligated all employers to make a good-faith attempt to verify that all workers hired on or after 6 November 1986 had authorisation to work by requiring their employees to fill out and complete what are called I-9 forms within three days of their hire.[43] As part of this process, employers must examine an employee's documents and certify that they have done so. IRCA imposed civil and criminal penalties (known as "employer sanctions") on employers who violated this process by *knowingly* hiring unauthorised workers. For the first time in US

40. US Select Commission on Immigration and Refugee Policy, *US Immigration Policy and the National Interest* (Final Report of the Commission) (Washington, DC: The Commission, 1981), pp. 46–47.

41. *Ibid.*, pp. 60, 82.

42. Calavita, "US Immigration and Policy Responses", *op. cit.*, pp. 66–68.

43. According to the federal government, I-9 forms are "used for verifying the identity and employment authorisation of individuals hired for employment in the United States." See <http://www.uscis.gov/portal/site/uscis/menuitem.5af9bb95919f35e66f614176543f6d1a/?vgnextoid=31b3ab0a43b5d010VgnVCM10000048f3d6a1RCRD&vgnextchannel=db029c7755cb9010VgnVCM10000045f3d6a1RCRD>.

history, the state directly restricted employers from hiring unauthorised immigrant workers.[44]

Growing the Apparatus of Control

During roughly the first half of the twentieth century, powerful agricultural interests played a significant role in producing and maintaining a yawning gap between US state rhetoric championing strong boundary and immigration policing, and actual practice. Thus, there appears to have been little serious political will among national political leaders, especially those from states abutting the US–Mexico divide, to fund boundary and immigration policing.[45] One result was that the INS, whose functions were absorbed into the Department of Homeland Security in 2002, would effectively open and shut the boundary depending on the needs of domestic economic interests. Despite the Border Patrol's charge to apprehend and exclude unauthorised migrants, "it seems that in practice the Border Patrol functioned primarily to regulate the numbers that were already in the country" during this period.[46]

The relatively weak provision of state resources for boundary enforcement continued during the 1960s and much of the 1970s when the number of permanent INS positions remained relatively constant, despite a very large increase in Border Patrol apprehension of unauthorised migrants. The Border Patrol's 1980 budget was only $77 million, less than that of Baltimore's city police department and far less than half that of Philadelphia at the time.[47] Thus, while attempts by the federal government to control the entry and residence of immigrants grew significantly over the first several decades of the twentieth century, these efforts were inconsistent and riddled with internal contradictions, especially in regards to unauthorised migrants from Mexico. The lack of effective state control over unauthorised immigration demonstrates that the US–Mexico border region was not pacified in large part due to the influence of economic actors whose goals often contradicted those of the federal government, or at least particular sectors of the state apparatus.

This is not to suggest, however, that boundary and immigrant policing merely served the interests of capital during this period, nor that enforcement was a mere show. What it demonstrates is that such policing is the outgrowth of the complex interplay of competing social actors—e.g. employers, law and order and/or opportunistic politicians, nativist groups within civil society, powerful individuals within various federal agencies—and that, to understand the relative success or failure of boundary policing (in relation to the officially stated goals),

44. Peter Brownell, "The Declining Enforcement of Employer Sanctions", *Migration Information Source*, 1 September 2005; Renée Suarez Congdon, "Comparing Employer Sanctions Provisions and Employment Eligibility Verification Procedures in the United States and the United Kingdom", *Indiana International & Comparative Law Review*, Vol. 18, No. 2 (2008), pp. 391–436; Kati L. Griffith, "A Supreme Stretch: The Supremacy Clause in the Wake of IRCA and Hoffman Plastic Compounds", *Cornell International Law Journal*, Vol. 41 (2008), pp. 127–138; Michael J. Wishnie, "Prohibiting the Employment of Unauthorised Immigrants: The Experiment Fails", *The University of Chicago Legal Forum* (2007), pp. 193–217.

45. See, for example, Galarza, *op. cit.*, p. 61.

46. Julian Samora, *Los Mojados: The Wetback Story* (Notre Dame and London: University of Notre Dame Press, 1971), p. 48. See also James D. Cockcroft, *Outlaws in the Promised Land: Mexican Immigrant Workers and America's Future* (New York: Grove Press, 1986); and Lytle Hernández, *op. cit.*

47. Calavita, "US Immigration and Policy Responses", *op. cit.*, p. 61.

we need to appreciate that interplay, and the contradictions and complementarities it embodies.

One person who embodies that complexity is Pete Wilson. A Republican, Wilson served as San Diego's mayor from December 1971 to January 1983. It was during his first year in office that Wilson coined San Diego's official moniker—"America's Finest City."[48] In January 1983, he became one of California's two US senators, a position in which he remained until 1991, after which he became California's governor, an office he held until the beginning of 1999.

Over the course of his political career, Wilson repeatedly championed immigration and boundary policing. While San Diego's mayor, he pressured the Carter administration in 1977, for instance, to provide federal assistance "in dealing with the economic and crime problems caused by the flood of illegal aliens," explained *The San Diego Union*.[49] In the mid-1980s, he called for the physical closure of the US–Mexico boundary if Mexican officials refused to cooperate with American efforts to stem the influx of unauthorised immigrants.[50] In early 1991, Governor Wilson blamed both legal and extralegal immigration for significantly contributing to a budget crisis in the State of California.[51] Later that same year, Wilson blamed the federal government for failing to compensate state and local governments adequately for costs related to immigration and for its failure to control unauthorised immigration across the US–Mexico boundary.[52] When Democrat Bill Clinton became US president in 1993, Wilson greatly escalated his anti-Washington rhetoric by castigating the federal government for failing to control the US–Mexico boundary and to appropriate billions of dollars promised (by the Reagan administration) for health, education and welfare services to immigrants—both legal and unauthorised.[53]

What was curious about Wilson's position is that he had played a key role while in the US Senate of undermining boundary and immigration enforcement. In 1983, for example, then-Senator Wilson co-authored legislation that disallowed the INS to raid farm fields without a judge's warrant. The provision became law in 1986 with the passage of IRCA and basically put a halt to INS farm checks.[54] On a number of other occasions, Wilson pressured INS officials to stop workplace raids on California companies. And in the late 1970s, he and his wife had employed an unauthorised migrant as their maid.[55]

---

48. Kelly Mayhew, *Under the Perfect Sun: The San Diego Tourists Never See* (New York: The New Press, 2005), p. 272. See also <http://www.sandiego.gov/>.

49. James Cary, "Carter Discusses Border Problems", *The San Diego Union*, 10 February 1977, p. A-1+.

50. Gerry Braun, "Wilson Would Close Border If … ", *The San Diego Union*, 22 August 1986, p. A-1+.

51. Sharon Spivak, "Wilson Blames Budget Woes on Unchecked Immigration", *San Diego Tribune*, 12 April 1991, p. A-1+.

52. Robert J. Caldwell, "Washington Is Shirking the Costs of Immigration" (op-ed), *The San Diego Union*, 29 September 1991, p. C-1+.

53. Peter Schrag, *Paradise Lost: California's Experience, America's Future* (New York: The New Press, 1998), p. 232.

54. Marcus Stern, "Back in '89, Pete Wilson Wasn't So Adamant about Migrant Issue", *The San Diego Union-Tribune*, 4 September 1993, p. A3; Marcus Stern, "In '83, Wilson Helped Curb INS Searches", *The San Diego Union-Tribune*, 17 September 1994, p. A-1+. This interpretation of the effect of the law proved to be valid when the author visited a strawberry farm in Watsonville in 1996. One of the owners informed the author that he had not seen the INS on his establishment in over 10 years. The owner speculated that at least 50 per cent of his employees were unauthorised migrants.

55. Paul Jacobs, "Wilson Often Battled INS, Letters Show", *Los Angeles Times*, 25 September 1995, p. A3.

While Pete Wilson's immigration politics showed a certain inconsistency, his efforts to highlight the putative fiscal and social costs of unauthorised immigration had a significant effect on national politics. Wilson undoubtedly played a significant role in pushing the Clinton administration towards a more restrictionist stance on boundary policing,[56] and in helping to bring about the dramatic infusion of policing-related resources that transformed the US–Mexico borderlands beginning in the early- to mid-1990s. Between Fiscal Year (FY) 1994 and the end of FY 2000, the number of Border Patrol agents expanded from 4,200 to 9,212. Meanwhile, the budget for immigration-related enforcement efforts along the south-west boundary grew from $400 million in FY 1993 to $800 million in FY 1997.[57]

What transpired in the 1990s was just a foreshadowing of far greater things to come—especially in the wake of the attacks of 11 September 2001. The FY 2003 budget provided a $2 billion *increase* for border policing,[58] most of which was dedicated to the south-west borderlands. As for the Border Patrol, the number of agents has more than doubled since 2000. As of 2013, there are more than 21,000 agents. In FY 2012, the combined budget of US Customs and Border Protection, the parent agency of the Border Patrol, Immigration and Customs Enforcement, or ICE (which focuses on immigration policing in the US interior), and a biometric tracking system called US VISIT totalled almost $18 billion.[59]

The transformation that began in the early to mid-1990s initially avoided the policing of workplaces. But with the ideological and material hardening and growth of the apparatus of exclusion and control embodied in that transformation, the workplace eventually became a target. This demonstrates the shifting nature of socio-territorial boundaries—as reflected in the intensification and spread of immigration policing to the US interior beyond locales within the US–Mexico borderlands, for example[60]—as well as the power of those boundaries and of those who construct them. It also manifests how state sovereignty is concerned not only with matters of territory and the associated boundaries, but with the regulation of bodies within and throughout the space of the territorial state, a project that involves the production of law-abiding citizens and excludable outsiders.[61] As political scientist Christopher H. Pyle wrote, "every bureaucracy is a solution in search of a problem, and if it can't find a problem to fit its solution, they will redefine the problem."[62] In other words, bureaucracies have a tendency to insert

56. Patricia King and Donna Foote, "Across the Borderline", *Newsweek*, 31 May 1993, p. 25; Fred Barnes, "No Entry: The Republicans' Immigration War", *The New Republic*, 8 November 1993, p. 10+; Ruth Conniff, "The War on Aliens", *The Progressive*, 22 October 1993, pp. 22–29; Andrew Murr, "A Nasty Turn on Immigrants", *Newsweek*, 23 August 1993, p. 28; Jeannette Money, "No Vacancy: The Political Geography of Immigration Control in Advanced Industrial Countries", *International Organization*, Vol. 51, No. 4 (1997), p. 697.

57. *Migration News*, November 1997, available: <http://migration.ucdavis.edu/mn/>.

58. Peter Andreas, *Border Games: Policing the U.S.-Mexico Divide* (Ithaca, NY: Cornell University Press, 2009), p. 154.

59. See Doris Meissner, Donald M. Kerwin, Muzaffar Chisti and Claire Bergeron, *Immigration Enforcement in the United States: The Rise of a Formidable Machinery* (Washington, DC: Migration Policy Institute, 2013).

60. See Mathew Coleman, "Immigration Geopolitics beyond the Mexico–US Border", *Antipode*, Vol. 39, No. 1 (2007), pp. 54–76; and Todd Miller, *Border Patrol Nation: Dispatches from the Front Lines of Homeland Security* (San Francisco, CA: City Lights Books/Open Media, 2014).

61. See Thomas Blom Hansen and Finn Stepputat, "Introduction", in Thomas Blom Hansen and Finn Stepputat (eds.), *Sovereign Bodies: Citizens, Migrants, and States in the Postcolonial World* (Princeton, NJ: Princeton University Press, 2005), pp. 1–36.

62. Christopher H. Pyle, "Edward Snowden and the Real Issues", *Counterpunch.org*, 13 June 2013.

themselves where they have not previously been. As the case of the immigrant policing apparatus in the United States suggests, this would seem to be especially true of bureaucracies charged with matters of the ever-elastic category of security.

Policing Worksites

Officially, workplace enforcement (inspection and monitoring of worksites for the employment of unauthorised labourers) was one of the central planks of the new boundary and immigration control strategy that emerged in the mid-1990s during the first half of the Clinton administration.[63] In reality, however, the strategy put much greater emphasis on high-profile policing measures along the boundary than on workplace enforcement. As of late 1997, for example, the INS had only 23 workplace inspectors in the San Diego area (13 of whom the INS added following the implementation of Operation Gatekeeper, a geographically focused, enhanced boundary policing strategy launched on 1 October 1994). In the Los Angeles district of the INS (an area comprising at the time a population of more than 20 million people), the INS issued only 18 "intent to fine" notices to employers for hiring extralegal migrants in FY 1996.[64] On a national scale, the number of fines levied against employers actually decreased from 2,000 in FY 1992 to 888 in FY 1997; the amount of fines levied decreased from $17 million to $8 million.[65] While INS arrests and deportations of non-criminal "illegal aliens" (apprehended through interior enforcement measures) increased in 1996 and 1997, they declined significantly in 1998 and 1999—arguably a manifestation of the strong US economy, the very low unemployment rate and the accompanying need of US employers for workers (especially low-wage ones). As *The New York Times* reported in March 2000, "[workplace] raids have all but stopped around the country over the last year." While crossing the boundary is harder than ever, the newspaper asserted, "once inside the country, illegal immigrants are now largely left alone." As such, according to a high-level official tasked with immigration and boundary policing matters, unauthorised immigrant workers faced little risk at that time "unless the employer turns a worker in, and employers usually do that only to break a union or prevent a strike or that kind of stuff."[66]

Overall, the period of 1988–2003 saw a significant decline in INS/ICE audits of employers.[67] Under the Obama administration (which took office in 2009), however, audits have increased markedly. They rose from 250 in FY 2007 to

63. "Remarks on the Immigration Policy Initiative and an Exchange with Reporters" and "Memorandum on Illegal Immigration", *Weekly Compilation of Presidential Documents*, Vol. 31, No. 6 (1995), pp. 199–204.

64. Robert Kahn, "Operation Gatekeeper", *Z Magazine*, Vol. 10, No. 12 (December 1997), pp. 14–16.

65. *Migration News*, November 1998, available: <http://migration.ucdavis.edu/mn/>; about 2,000 US employers were participating in 1998 in the INS's voluntary Basic Pilot Program, under which the Social Security Administration and the INS verified the social security and immigration numbers of all newly hired workers. As a reward for cooperation, participating companies were immune from INS raids. Given that many unauthorised immigrants were able to borrow legal documents from friends or relatives or obtain fraudulent documents, the programme had the unintended effect of sheltering unauthorised immigrants from INS enforcement (Laurie P. Cohen, "Free Ride: With Help from INS, US Meatpacker Taps Mexican Work Force", *The Wall Street Journal*, 15 October 1998, p. A1).

66. Louis Uchitelle, "INS Is Looking the Other Way as Illegal Immigrants Fill Jobs", *The New York Times*, 9 March 2000, p. A1.

67. Brownell, *op. cit.*; Wishnie, *op. cit.*

more than 3,000 in 2012, a time during which the United States experienced a significant economic downturn. Meanwhile, in the period between FYs 2009 and 2012, the amount of fines grew from $1 million to almost $13 million.[68]

More important, however, than the increase or decrease in workplace-related policing was the very fact that IRCA had made the knowing employment of unauthorised immigrants a crime. This provided a key component of the ideological, legal, political and, eventually, logistical foundation needed to make possible what happened in relation to the French Gourmet. In other words, by criminalising the knowing employment of those without a federal government-sanctioned right to work, IRCA provides a law-based justification for growth in workplace policing. In this regard, the law serves as a standard of behaviour not only for those intended as its targets, but also for those charged with upholding it, and the body politic as a whole.

This helps illustrate how and why the I-9 process, despite having many problems from the beginning of its implementation in 1987—most notably due to employer abuse and the counterfeiting and fraudulent use of documents—helped to open the door for more workplace-intrusive measures. The problems contributed to an assessment by the US Commission on Immigration Reform (1990–1997) of the employer sanctions system as ineffective. "[R]educing the employment magnet is the linchpin of a comprehensive strategy to reduce illegal immigration," stated the Commission in its 1994 report. To achieve such a reduction—and decrease the likelihood of fraud or discrimination by employers against authorised workers whose appearance or name is deemed "foreign"—the Commission recommended the establishment of a computerised registry that drew on data from the Social Security Registry and the INS, calling it "the most promising option for secure, non-discriminatory verification."[69] Hence, it sought to strengthen the system of workplace policing, not abolish it.

Out of the Commission's recommendations emerged language in the Illegal Immigration Reform and Immigrant Responsibility Act (IIRIRA), signed into law by President Bill Clinton in 1996, which eventually gave birth to E-Verify. IIRIRA required the testing of three different electronic screening programmes. Of the three, a system called the Basic Pilot Program proved to be the most viable and was implemented in 1997. Initially, it operated on a trial basis in five US states, with a sixth state added in 1999, and it remained a very small initiative, involving fewer than 5,000 employers until 2005. It was around this time that the G.W. Bush administration took a series of steps to strengthen and promote the programme, renaming it E-Verify in 2007.[70]

Free to use by employers, E-Verify does not replace the I-9 process. Rather, the electronic system is a complement to the paper one. As one analyst explains, "E-Verify gives employers a tool to detect false IDs and to avoid unknowingly employing an unauthorised immigrant." This is because "most fraudulent documents cannot be matched to a valid record in the Social Security or Department

68. Valdes, *op. cit.*

69. See US Commission on Immigration Reform, *Executive Summary* (1994), available: <http://www.utexas.edu/lbj/uscir/exesum94.pdf>.

70. Micah Bump, "Immigration, Technology, and the Worksite: The Challenges of Electronic Employment Verification", *Georgetown Immigration Law Journal*, Vol. 22, No. 3 (2008), pp. 391–404; Rosenblum, *op. cit.*; see also the "History and Milestones" section of the E-Verify areas of the US Citizenship and Immigration Services website, available: <http://www.uscis.gov/portal/site/uscis>.

of Homeland Security databases" that serve as the sources of verifying information for the programme. In FY 2009, employers used E-Verify to exclude approximately 166,000 unauthorised workers.[71]

According to one estimate, approximately three-quarters of unauthorised workers use fraudulent documents for purposes of employment.[72] E-Verify cannot detect all fraudulent documents—only fake ones. The system is vulnerable, for example, to a worker's use of valid identity documents borrowed or stolen from another person. Similarly, E-Verify cannot tell when an employer circumvents the system by simply not screening a particular hire, or by hiring someone "off the books."[73] While these are obvious shortcomings of the system, they also facilitate a proverbial silver lining from the perspective of the champions of the homeland security state: like the insufficiently robust I-9 system, they pave the way for even more intrusive measures of "security" aimed at cleansing worksites throughout the United States of unauthorised employees.

Transforming the Territorial State

In terms of its "home" within the federal bureaucracy, the regulation of immigration in the United States has shifted considerably since the late 1800s. When the Chinese Exclusion Act was passed in 1882, immigration policing was housed within the Department of the Treasury. It shifted in 1903 to the (no-longer-existing) Department of Commerce and Labour, and, following that, to the then-newly established Department of Labour in 1913. In 1940, the INS (which was created in 1933) moved to the Department of Justice where it stayed until 2003 when it was dismantled and its functions absorbed into the Department of Homeland Security.

These shifts across time have accompanied a steady, and—over the last two decades—dramatic, strengthening of the boundary and enforcement apparatus in the United States since the 1880s. They also seem to mimic the dominant manners in which the state (admittedly, an internally differentiated one) perceives immigrants over time. From seeing them first and foremost as labourers and commodified bodies, to treating migrants as subjects of the law, to now perceiving immigrants, in many ways at least, foremost as security concerns (today the Border Patrol defines its "priority mission" as "preventing terrorists and terrorists' weapons, including weapons of mass destruction, from entering the United States") the "migration" of immigrant regulation within the federal bureaucracy constitutes a growing securitisation of immigrant bodies and of the state.

The state, political sociologist Michael Mann reminds us, is a messy concept.[74] Still, in terms of the modern territorial state, all of them share basic functions, one being the control of mobility across the boundaries that delimit national territory—that is, the modern state claims an absolute right to regulate whom (and what) enters and leaves its territory, a "monopoly of the legitimate means of

71. Rosenblum, *op. cit.*, p. 5.

72. *Ibid.*

73. *Ibid.*

74. Michael Mann, "The Autonomous Power of the State: Its Origins, Mechanisms and Results", *European Archive of Sociology*, Vol. 25 (1984), pp. 185–213.

movement."[75] It is from this key state function that boundaries, passports, visas and other aspects of the policing apparatus, such as E-Verify, emerge.

What underlies the state's power, suggests Zygmunt Bauman, is human uncertainty and vulnerability—phenomena embodied by, among allegedly threatening others, the stranger or immigrant. It is, he writes, "against those twin, hotly resented yet constant accompaniments of the human condition, and against the fear and anxiety they tend to generate, that the modern state has promised to protect its subjects."[76] It is from this promise, and its practices to achieve it, that the state derives much of its legitimacy and ability to command the obedience of the citizenry.

In a modern capitalist society, so-called market forces contribute greatly to the production of uncertainty and vulnerability. Helping to limit the citizenry's exposure to market-related insecurities is one way by which a state can establish its legitimacy. In an era characterised by, among other processes, neoliberalism, however, state mechanisms of social security have eroded and regulatory tools that restrain business activities have diminished, one effect being a weakening of state legitimacy. As such, argues Bauman, the state "must seek other, non-economic varieties of vulnerability and uncertainty on which to rest its legitimacy." One manner by which many states (and certainly the United States) have done so is by emphasising what Bauman calls "the issue of *personal safety*: current or portending, overt or hidden, genuine or putative fears of the *threats to human bodies, possessions and habitats*."[77] The terrorist, the so-called criminal alien, and unauthorised migrants who "steal" jobs from their allegedly rightful citizen owners are contemporary embodiments of those personalised threats to human bodies (of a national citizen type) and their belongings writ large.

The rise in the emphasis on personal security both reflects and helps to produce a state bureaucracy charged with protecting it. In the case of the United States and the emergence of E-Verify, this state bureaucracy is perhaps best demonstrated by the emergence and rapid growth of the Department of Homeland Security, and by the dramatic expansion of the immigration and boundary policing apparatus more broadly—an expansion that increasingly coerces the private sector to participate in the policing,[78] thus further blurring the already fuzzy state–society boundary.[79] If, as Bauman asserts, uncertainty and vulnerability are the foundation of modern state power, it would seem to follow that those within the state apparatus charged with guarding against what dominant state sectors frame as priority manifestations of such would enjoy an inordinate amount of power. In this regard, what many call the "securitisation" of immigration control in the United States and its increasing spread to the workplace is hardly surprising.

The securitisation–immigration and boundary control nexus is certainly not limited to the United States; nor can one explain the rise of this paradigm by

---

75. John Torpey, *The Invention of the Passport: Surveillance, Citizenship and the State* (Cambridge: Cambridge University Press, 2000), p. 1.

76. Zygmunt Bauman, *Collateral Damage: Social Inequalities in a Global Age* (Cambridge: Polity Press, 2011), p. 52.

77. *Ibid.*, p. 54; emphasis original.

78. Huyen Pham, "The Private Enforcement of Immigration Laws", *The Georgetown Law Journal*, Vol. 96 (2008), pp. 777–826.

79. Timothy Mitchell, "The Limits of the State: Beyond Statist Approaches and their Critics", *American Political Science Review*, Vol. 85, No. 1 (1991), pp. 77–96.

pointing solely at the rise of neoliberalised states and the retreat of collective measures of social security. There are myriad reasons for the hardening of territorial boundaries that has taken place over the last few decades—especially along the perimeters of relatively wealthy and privileged countries. These include an increasing blurring of the distinction between internal and international security; a concomitant production of a range of perceived threats and a general sense of unease within national citizenries; and the criminalisation of unauthorised migrants—a phenomenon that dovetails with neoliberalism to the extent that it emphasises individual responsibility as it articulates with law-breaking while obscuring the structural factors that underlie migration; and the rise of an "industrial complex" in the realm of immigration and boundary control that helps to drive its own growth and spread.[80] Still, by "performing" the boundary—whether in the US–Mexico borderlands or in workplaces within the United States—the state provides a semblance of fulfilling its duties, at least in part, while helping to legitimate its very existence.

Within the workplace, the growing enforcement web has the effect of "disciplining" labour by decreasing the likelihood that employees without proper papers will challenge substandard working conditions for fear of arrest and deportation.[81] Such fear is well founded: according to a 2000 study, 52 per cent of companies where union drives were taking place in the United States at the time threatened to call US immigration authorities if the organising campaign involved unauthorised migrants.[82]

Defenders of measures such as E-Verify argue that such outcomes make it all the more necessary that workplace policing be consistent across national space. In other words, were all employers required to use E-Verify, none would be able to use the threat of arrest and deportation to undercut unionisation efforts. This would have the added benefit, so goes the argument, of protecting native, or citizen, workers from unfair competition by unauthorised workers.

There are at least four important factors that such arguments ignore. First are the limits of the state's capacity to police worksites and thus to eliminate unauthorised employees. This is due in no small part to the desire and ability of capital to weaken the state's ability to police businesses, and to widen the gap between the law on paper and the law in practice. In Italy, for instance—although in recent years there has been an increasing criminalisation of employment of unauthorised workers employer sanctions laws[83]—it appears that, due to pressures from business owners, employer sanctions are rarely enforced, and inconsistently so.[84]

80. Jesse Jr. Díaz, "Immigration Policy, Criminalization and the Growth of the Immigration Industrial Complex: Restriction, Expulsion, and Eradication of Undocumented in the US", *Western Criminology Review*, Vol. 12, No. 2 (2011), pp. 35–54. See also Miller, *op cit.*

81. Regarding how undocumented status often inhibits the propensity of workers to make claims upon their employers, see Shannon Gleeson, "Labor Rights for All? The Role of Undocumented Immigrant Status for Worker Claims Making", *Law & Social Inquiry*, Vol. 35, No. 3 (2010), pp. 561–602.

82. Kate Brofenbrenner, "Uneasy Terrain: The Impact of Capital Mobility on Workers, Wages, and Union Organizing", report submitted to the US Trade Deficit Review Commission (2000), available: <http://digitalcommons.ilr.cornell.edu/reports/1/>. See also David Bacon, *Illegal People: How Globalization Creates Migration and Criminalizes Immigrants* (Boston, MA: Beacon Press, 2008); Nicholas De Genova, *Working the Boundaries: Race, Space, and "Illegality" in Mexican Chicago* (Durham, NC: Duke University Press, 2005).

83. See, for example, Matthew Carr, *Fortress Europe: Dispatches from a Gated Continent* (New York: New Press, 2012), p. 183.

84. Kitty Calavita, *Immigrants at the Margins: Law, Race, and Exclusion in Southern Europe* (Cambridge: Cambridge University Press, 2005).

Of course, the relationship between capital and the state is hardly a static one, nor is it equal across nation-states. Among members of the European Union, for example, there appears to be significant unevenness in terms of the relative strength of worker policing regimes. Yet even when such regimes are relatively robust—this is the second factor—employers can, and many certainly will, circumvent the apparatus of control and employ unauthorised workers in an informal manner.

Take the United Kingdom, for instance, where, curiously, debate about employer sanctions did not begin until the late 1970s—an idea that was abandoned, for a complex set of reasons, and not taken up again until the 1990s. It was through a combination of internal and external pressures (the European Union, most of whose member states had employer sanctions provisions by the mid-1990s, pushed for a harmonisation of approaches to the employment of unauthorised workers) that the UK adopted the Asylum and Immigration Appeals Act of 1996, which contained the country's first employer sanctions provision.[85] Over time, regulations and policing, as in the European Union as a whole,[86] have strengthened: in 2008, legislation went into effect that makes it a civil violation to employ an unauthorised worker, with employers facing fines of up to £10,000 per worker if it can be shown that the employer failed to carry out a document check to ensure that a job applicant has authorisation to work in the country. Employers who *knowingly* give work to "illegal workers" face up to two years in prison and a fine of an "unlimited" amount.[87] Employers are required to ascertain the eligibility of all would-be employees to work by ensuring that they have at least one document deemed by the state to be valid for such purposes.[88] Still, as in the case of the United States, employers are able to circumvent this system by simply hiring individuals "off the books," which becomes a reason, of course, for greater levels of policing—at least from the perspective of the state.

The third factor relates to the resiliency and determination of unauthorised migrant workers themselves. Even in the face of rather draconian regimes of policing and exclusion, "illegal" migrants continue to arrive and reside in inhospitable countries, and unauthorised workers continue to seek employment. In Malaysia, for example, the government since 2005 has employed a strike force—one that grew out of a civilian militia group that had been created in the 1960s to fight against alleged communists—to hunt down unauthorised residents and workers. (Most of them come from Indonesia, with many others coming from Bangladesh, Burma/Myanmar, India, Nepal and Vietnam.) The group's leaders carry arms, and its deputised members have the right to enter homes or search people on the street without a warrant. Called Rela, the force has (as of 2007) nearly half a million volunteer members, more than the total number within the country's military and police forces. Their arrestees face up to five years in prison and a whipping of up to six strokes. Human rights groups accuse Rela members of violence,

85. Congdon, *op cit.*, pp. 404–405.

86. Carr, *op cit.*, p. 125.

87. See <https://www.gov.uk/penalties-for-employing-illegal-workers>.

88. See UK Border Agency, *Full Guide for Employers on Preventing Illegal Workers in the UK* (London: UK Border Agency, Immigration Group, May 2012), available: <https://www.gov.uk/check-an-employees-right-to-work-documents>.

extortion, theft and illegal detention.[89] Yet it appears that hundreds of thousands of unauthorised employees continue to labour in Malaysia.[90]

In all these scenarios, the employers have their control over their workforce enhanced given the always-looming threat of deportation for at least some workers. Simultaneously, these contexts and practices produce "precarious" or "ideal" workers—ones desirable to capital due to their heightened exploitability. Just as enhanced boundary enforcement, in filtering out older and physically weaker migrants, helps to create, in the words of communication scholar Michael Huspek, "the perfect workers,"[91] immigration controls broadly produce various forms of labour, among them workers who will tolerate (because they have little choice) low-wage, insecure employment with long hours—at least for a limited period of time.[92] They also help to produce precarious spaces—from those of individual worksites to that of national territory as a whole—ones that are increasingly policed and those working within them increasingly suspect.[93]

This speaks to how precarious or ideal workers are produced at various sites, the French Gourmet in San Diego being one, as well as at different geographic scales. As discussed earlier, for example, some local states—such as Arizona and Mississippi—have required that all employers within the state use E-Verify. One might consider this a variant of (national) "statecraft from below,"[94] as a well as a variant of immigration policing through "the backdoor"[95] in that it serves as an example of how local states effectively force the hand of the national state, holding it accountable in effect to the standards it sets (but might fail to uphold) and build it and its geographic practices and expressions in the process. In this regard, geographic scales, such as the local and the national, are incestuous: while perhaps analytically distinct, in practice they flow from and produce one another.

Finally—and this is the fourth matter—arguments in favour of E-Verify-like policing tools help to normalise nation-statism and its practices of exclusion, and typically avoid matters of ethics and human rights that would challenge national socio-territorial boundaries. They thus help to reproduce a profoundly unequal and fundamentally unjust world order, one deeply divided along the intersecting axes of race, class and nation. It is a world order that some scholars have characterised as one of global apartheid,[96] one reason being that countries regulate mobility

89. Seth Mydans, "Foreign Workers Face Campaign of Brutality in Malaysia", *International Herald Tribune*, 9 December 2007.

90. See Abhrajit Gangopadhyay and Jason Ng, "Malaysia Launches Immigration Operation to Deport Illegal Workers", *The Wall Street Journal*, 1 September 2013.

91. Michael Kahn, "Production of State, Capital, and Citizenry", *Social Justice*, Vol. 28, No. 2 (2001), pp. 51–68.

92. Bridget Anderson, "Migration, Immigration Controls and the Fashioning of Precarious Workers", *Work, Employment & Society*, Vol. 24, No. 2 (2010), pp. 300–317; Harrison and Lloyd, *op. cit.*

93. Josiah McC. Heyman, "Why Interdiction? Immigration Control at the United States–Mexico Border", *Regional Studies*, Vol. 33, No. 7 (1999), pp. 619–630; Josiah McC. Heyman, "United States Surveillance over Mexican Lives at the Border: Snapshots of an Emerging Regime", *Human Organization*, Vol. 58, No. 4 (1999), pp. 429–437.

94. Roxanne L. Doty, "The Double-Writing of Statecraft: Exploring State Responses to Illegal Immigration", *Alternatives*, No. 21 (1996), pp. 171–189.

95. Monica Varsanyi, "Immigration Policing through the Backdoor: City Ordinances, the 'Right to the City,' and the Exclusion of Undocumented Day Laborers", *Urban Geography*, Vol. 29, No. 1 (2008), pp. 29–52.

96. See, for example, Simon Dalby, "Globalisation or Global Apartheid? Boundaries and Knowledge in Postmodern Times", in David Newman (ed.), *Boundaries, Territory, and Postmodernity* (London: Frank

and residence on, among other factors, the basis of geographic origins—one of the foundations of supposed racial distinctions. In doing so, nation-states not only limit the rights and protections afforded to migrants because of an essentialised characteristic over which they have no control, they also uphold a world order in which resources (broadly defined), and the right to have access to those resources (through mobility, residence and employment) are unequally distributed. They thus help to shape the life and death circumstances of many of the planet's denizens, while drawing upon and reproducing systematic violence and, hence, what is effectively dehumanisation.

Conclusion

As of August 2014, the legislative fate of what is called "comprehensive immigration reform" (CIR) in the United States is unclear. That said, if and when any CIR bill ultimately does win Congressional approval, it appears that an enhanced version of E-Verify, one that will be mandatory for all employers across the country, will be a central component of the legislation. Indeed, E-Verify is the most popular component of the multifaceted immigration reform package among the US public.[97] But whether or not CIR ultimately passes, there is little doubt that efforts to implement E-Verify-like measures, and more intrusive work-site and employee policing in relation to immigration law, are the wave of the foreseeable future in the United States.

To the extent that such efforts are successful, the effects of that wave are manifold, one of which is that of increased violence of a structural nature—the sort that damages human relations and harms individuals and communities—one that contravenes an expansive notion of human rights.[98] In the case of the French Gourmet, the federal government ultimately deported many of the arrested workers. According to a 2011 email from Lauren Mack, a spokesperson for Immigration and Customs Enforcement, nine of what the agency refers to as the "illegal alien bakery workers" had been deported by that time. More than three years after the arrests, another seven were still in "immigration proceedings"—in other words ICE was trying to "remove" them, but the individuals were contesting their deportation orders. And two were allowed to stay for serving as "material witnesses" in the case against the French Gourmet. An employee of the French Gourmet spoke to the human impact of these "removals" when he wrote in 2012, "I think the saddest part about this whole story is the way that the undocumented workers were manipulated by the feds in the pursuit of the case. Many of them were my close coworkers and watching them disappear made me sick to my stomache [sic]."[99]

Cass, 1999), pp. 132–150; Nevins, *Operation Gatekeeper and Beyond, op. cit.*; Nandita Sharma, *Home Economics: Nationalism and the Making of "Migrant Workers" in Canada* (Toronto: University of Toronto Press, 2006).

97. Mark Trumbell, "US Immigration Reform: Why 'E-Verify' Screenings, While Flawed, Will Pass", *The Christian Science Monitor*, 7 June 2013.

98. See Joseph Nevins, "Thinking Out of Bounds: A Critical Analysis of Academic and Human Rights Writings on Migrant Deaths in the US–Mexico Border Region", *Migraciones Internacionales*, Vol. 2, No. 2 (2003), pp. 171–190; Joseph Nevins, *Dying to Live: A Story of US Immigration in an Age of Global Apartheid* (San Francisco, CA: Open Media/City Lights Books, 2008).

99. This is the result of an exchange of emails initiated by the worker after he read a 2011 blog post on the French Gourmet written by the author. See <https://nacla.org/blog/2011/10/19/right-work-all>.

Such an outcome demonstrates how violence and anti-violence (in the form of efforts to reduce what are framed as violent threats) often go hand in hand in the territorialised nation-state. As political scientist Jenny Edkins has written, "In modern political communities in the west, our faith in the social order and our search for security are invested in systems that themselves are productive of and produced by force and violence." As such, the modern state is a bundle of contradictions: "a promise of safety, security and meaning alongside a reality of abuse, control and coercion."[100] This "reality of abuse, control, and coercion" is certainly true for those defined as outside the socio-political-geographical boundaries of wealthy and powerful states. Security for those from within necessitates—especially in a world of deep socio-economic inequality—the production of insecurity for those from without. The making of this security–insecurity nexus is inextricably tied to the wide disparity in the effective availability of freedom of movement across the globe, a freedom inextricably tied to the right to work, one enshrined in, among other international documents and conventions, the Universal Declaration of Human Rights, Article 23 of which states that "Everyone has the right to work, to free choice of employment, to just and favourable conditions of work, and to protection against unemployment" and "to just and favourable remuneration ensuring for himself and his family an existence worthy of human dignity."[101] That the US government effectively denied this right to workers at the French Gourmet is the embodiment of violence. It serves as a reminder of border scholars James Anderson's and Liam O'Dowd's suggestion that territorial boundaries typically grow out of violence or the threat of force.[102]

It is a violence that is both reflective and productive of the modern territorial state—and increasingly so in the case of the United States—vis-à-vis unauthorised territorial boundary crossers, workers and residents. At the same time, it is a manifestation of the state's decreasing role in protecting workers' rights to biophysical wellbeing, as demonstrated by a marked decline in worksite safety monitoring by the federal government,[103] and their right to unionise and represent their interests through collective action.[104] Thus, instead of concentrating on threats from "within"—those posed by capital and abusive employers, for instance—the state focuses its gaze and practice on alleged threats from "without." In other words, the state increasingly polices the relatively weak—in the case of the French Gourmet, unauthorised workers paid the highest price—while ignoring workplace safety matters and labour rights. Were the state to provide protection to all workers labouring within national territory—regardless of citizenship or immigration status—it would not only make unauthorised workers less "perfect" or "ideal" (in addition to precarious), but it would also prove a far more effective means of ensuring worker wellbeing.[105] That the state does not do so speaks to its priorities,

100. Jenny Edkins, *Trauma and the Memory of Politics* (Cambridge: Cambridge University Press, 2003), p. 6.

101. Available online at: <www.un.org/en/documents/udhr/>.

102. James Anderson and Liam O'Dowd, "Borders, Border Regions and Territoriality: Contradictory Meanings, Changing Significance", *Regional Studies*, Vol. 33, No. 7 (1999), pp. 593–604.

103. Michelle Chen, "When Safety Becomes Voluntary: Workplace Self-Policing Program Under Scrutiny", *In These Times*, 10 July 2012; Mike Elk, "The Texas Fertilizer Plant Explosion Cannot Be Forgotten", *The Washington Post*, 23 April 2013.

104. See Human Rights Watch, *Discounting Rights: Wal-Mart's Violation of US Workers' Right to Freedom of Association* (New York: Human Rights Watch, 2007).

105. Wishnie, *op. cit.* For an interesting discussion of how unions can and sometimes do limit the harmful reach of the state and create "enclaves of rights" in the process, see Parks, *op cit.*

changing internal structure and the shifting ways in which it relates to various constituencies and its internally differentiated citizenry, and those who reside within what it defines as its national territory.

Acknowledgements

I thank Larry Herzog for inviting me to submit a manuscript for consideration to this special issue, and for his constructive feedback on the first full version of the manuscript. I also extend my gratitude to the two anonymous reviewers for their careful readings and valuable comments on a subsequent iteration. Finally, I am indebted to Kaitlin Reed for extensive editorial and research support, and critical feedback on various versions of the manuscript.

Solving the Border Paradox? Border Security, Economic Integration and the Mérida Initiative

PAUL ASHBY

Since the period of negotiations for and signing of the North American Free Trade Agreement (NAFTA), the United States has focused policy efforts towards Mexico on two macro-goals: deepening economic integration and increasing border security. This article contends that these two goals appear to be paradoxical. It shows that cross-border economic interaction has grown alongside a discursive and hard policy focus on US border security policies to meet various "threats." Engaging with policy detail of the Mérida Initiative, it argues that the US aims to overcome this paradox by treating the whole NAFTA area as a shared economic and security space, and pushing concepts of "homeland security" beyond its frontiers. The article concludes that this is a challenging undertaking.

Introduction and Outline

Mexico is in the midst of a security crisis. Despite an apparent (relative) improvement in statistics for homicide, and a public rebranding exercise by the recently elected Partido Revolucionario Institucional (PRI) administration of Enrique Peña Nieto,[1] large areas of the country remain gripped by insecurity and violence commonly associated with the illegal drug business and the activities of the powerful drug trafficking groups that engage in it. While Mexico has long experienced violence associated with drug smuggling, in December 2006 former President Calderón launched a militarised crackdown on drug traffickers which has coincided with a staggering increase in carnage, leaving potentially upwards of 120,000 to 130,000 dead.[2] The US, through policy and aid commitments making up and associated with the Mérida Initiative, has focused a good deal of attention

1. Mexico's murder rate has dropped from its height in 2010 and 2011, not least due to falling figures in Ciudad Juárez, Chihuahua, which became the world leader in city homicides during those years. However, accurate statistics are hard to produce and find (see note 2).

2. Giving an accurate figure for drug-related homicides is extremely difficult, given high levels of impunity in Mexico. The various government database figures for homicides tied to organised crime are therefore extremely suspect in their assertions of detail. I use the numbers of Molly Molloy, who has paid unrivalled attention to this issue and uses the *overall* homicide figures provided by the Instituto Nacional de Estadística y Geografía (INEGI; http://www.inegi.org.mx) in her tally. This means that murders not strictly "drug related" may be captured in the total, but this is preferable to undercounting by relying on data provided by the government. See Molly Molloy, "The Mexican Undead: Towards a New History of the 'Drug War' Killing Fields", *Small Wars Journal* (21 August 2013), available: <http://smallwarsjournal.com/jrnl/art/the-mexican-undead-toward-a-new-history-of-the-"drug-war"-killing-fields> (accessed 11 August, 2014).

and support towards aiding the Mexican state tackle insecurity within its territory. Despite limited evidence for violence leaping the south-west border (hereafter "the border") on a large scale, Mexico's travails with drug-related instability have become part of a deeper debate on border security within the US, both in terms of actual US policy, and policy/academic discussion. Immigration, drug trafficking and terrorism have animated new rounds of border security crackdowns. These three concerns now co-exist in both discourse and, more importantly, policy. I highlight this development in the first section of the article.

The discussion then goes on to demonstrate how US border security efforts have led to the existence of a "border paradox." This argument draws on concepts well established by US–Mexico border scholars. As Andreas has noted, two seemingly contradictory trends have dominated US–Mexican bilateral relations (and US policy towards Mexico) since Mexico began to open its economy in the 1980s: the push towards deeper economic integration encompassing greatly enhanced and facilitated cross-border flows in finance and trade (culminating in the North American Free Trade Agreement [NAFTA]) as part of a drive towards North American economic integration, and the steep rise in US efforts to secure the border.[3] However, the emphasis on border security has sat uneasily with an integrated North American economy, and the former has impacted negatively on the latter, especially in terms of efficiency in border trade and bilateral cooperation. US border policy and its wider relationship with Mexico has been termed "schizophrenic," with seemingly mutually opposed agendas being pursued simultaneously, often driven by competing interest groups.[4] These trends have left us with the "paradoxical end result" of "both a borderless economy and a barricaded border."[5] I examine some of the key analysis of this border paradox from scholars of US–Mexican relations. The irony is that economic integration has generated or magnified its *own* security threats, which have inspired further border security initiatives, which in turn have further detrimental impacts on integration. In this way, the NAFTA zone can be seen in the light of increasing academic and US policy concern with the "dark side of globalisation" – the empowerment of illicit actors within interconnected economies that has put stress upon "traditional" sovereign borders.[6]

The figure of 130,000 does not include missing people, and these figures also do not take into account the dead and missing since publication dates.

3. Peter Andreas, *Border Games: Policing the US–Mexico Divide* (2nd edition) (New York: Cornell Publishing, 2009), pp. 4–5; Peter Andreas, "A Tale of Two Borders: The US–Canada and US–Mexico Lines after 9/11", in Peter Andreas and Thomas J. Biersteckeer (eds.), *The Rebordering of North America: Integration and Exclusion in a New Security Context* (London: Routledge, 2003), pp. 4 and 11.

4. Andrew Selee and Alberto Díaz-Cayeros, "The Dynamics of US–Mexican Relations", in Peter H. Smith and Andrew Selee (eds.), *Mexico and the United States: The Politics of Partnership* (Boulder, CO: Lynne Rienner Publishers, 2013), p. 50.

5. Andreas, "A Tale of Two Borders", *op. cit.*, p. 4.

6. Michael Miklaucic and Jacqueline Brewer, "Introduction", in Michael Miklaucic and Jacqueline Brewer, *Convergence: Illicit Networks and National Security in the Age of Globalization* (Washington, DC: National Defense University Press, 2013), pp. xiii–xxi; Nils Gilman, Jesse Goldhammer and Steven Weber (eds.), *Deviant Globalization: Black Market Economy in the 21st Century* (New York: The Continuum International Publishing Group, 2011); H. Richard Friman and Peter Andreas (eds.), *The Illicit Global Economy and State Power* (Lanham, MD: Rowman & Littlefield Publishers, 1999); Moisés Naím, *Illicit: How Smugglers, Traffickers and Copycats are Hijacking the Global Economy* (New York: Anchor Books, 2006); Jorge Heine and Ramesh Thakur, "Introduction: Globalization and Transnational Uncivil Society", in Jorge Heine and Ramesh Thakur, *The Dark Side of Globalization* (New York: United Nations University Press, 2011), pp. 1–16.

I use this work to build the second key argument of this article. Many of the analysts cited have seen economic integration and security as *competing* trends at the border. I argue, however, that this underplays the intractable association between US economic and security concerns. Indeed, deeper bilateral economic integration necessitates a deeper security focus, as Mexico's importance to wider US interests in continued economic prosperity and competiveness increases. After briefly analysing how various scholars have conceptualised this, I show that US policymakers and institutions themselves are well aware of this dilemma, and have attempted to formulate workable solutions that maintain the advantage of economic interaction while securing that interaction from potential threats. To this end, US policy has coalesced around concepts of border security projection, transnational organised crime (TOC) and the Mérida Initiative aid programme. Engaging with this policy can help us to understand that the US is attempting to alleviate the negative effects of economic integration and the "border paradox" by assisting Mexico to meet security threats before they reach the nation's boundary. Essentially, Mexican security has more than ever become US security within NAFTA, which has interesting ramifications for traditional views of border spaces. This development is underplayed in the existing literature. I use a brief discussion of policy detail to reinforce this case. However, we should make clear that this is a *nascent* approach that is itself bedevilled by challenges. I conclude, therefore, by discussing how the US–Mexico border region may remain both an economic interface and a site of heightened security.

Mexico's Security Crisis and Border Security

Mexico's security crisis spectacularly exploded into wider consciousness in recent years, but it has deeper roots in Mexico's history, and the history of narcotics and narcotics control.[7] Mexico has for some time been a transit country for drugs destined for the lucrative US market, but the opportunities for increased deliveries of and profits from drugs increased dramatically as US authorities cracked down on Caribbean shipment routes in the 1980s, moving the trade through the obvious alternative of a country with a 2,000 mile border with the desired final destination. This activity often centred around key border entry points, which already had the infrastructure for licit trade and a long history of illicit smuggling, and now had increasing opportunities to build on this established pattern as bilateral trade levels rose in the 1980s.[8] The 1994 passage of NAFTA inculcated a trade boom, creating further drug smuggling opportunities within greatly increased

7. Some helpful histories of narcotics smuggling, narcotics interdiction and US and Mexican involvement in both include Tom Feiling, *The Candy Machine: How Cocaine Took Over the World* (London: Penguin, 2009); Douglas Valentine, *The Strength of the Wolf: The Secret History of America's War on Drugs* (London: Verso, 2006); Paul Kenny and Mónica Serrano, "The Mexican State and Organised Crime: An Unending Story", in Paul Kenny and Monica Serrano (eds.) with Arturo Sotomayor, *Mexico's Security Failure: Collapse into Criminal Violence* (Abingdon: Routledge, 2012), pp. 29–53; Paul Kenny and Mónica Serrano, "Transition to Dystopia", in *ibid.*, pp. 54–85; Peter Watt and Roberto Zepeda, *Drug War Mexico: Politics, Neoliberalism and Violence in the New Narcoeconomy* (London: Zed Books, 2012).

8. See Howard Campbell, *Drug War Zone: Frontline Dispatches from the Streets of El Paso and Juárez* (Austin, TX: University of Texas Press, 2009) for a fascinating and indicative account of how busy border cities became hubs for smuggling of all kinds, through alcohol during prohibition to drugs (and much else in between).

cross-border journeys and cargo. These developments overlapped with (and were related to) seismic social shifts, including severe economic recessions, large economically driven population migrations and the unravelling and end of the 71-year single party rule of the PRI that culminated with the election of the Partido Acción Nacional (PAN) in 2000. Violence connected to increasingly competitive "drug cartels" began to creep up, especially in certain border cities like Ciudad Juárez, Tijuana and Nuevo Laredo. In 2005, PAN president Vicente Fox ordered a military crackdown after spectacular street violence in Nuevo Laredo. In December 2006, newly and controversially elected Felipe Calderón, also of the PAN, launched a "war" against these groups in the context of violence in several Mexican states, especially his home state of Michoacán.[9]

The recent uptick in drug-related violence is a widespread phenomenon, and has had various "hotspots"—the heroin and smuggling "kingpin" producing mountains of Sinaloa,[10] rural Michoacán and Guerrero, port cities like Veracruz and Acapulco, even the commercial hub of Monterrey. However, barring naval shipping routes, the drugs travelling to the United States cross the border. They often do so at aforementioned border entry points such as Nuevo Laredo–Laredo, Ciudad Juárez–El Paso and Tijuana–San Diego. As a result of this geographical "advantage," these areas have often become focal points for drug-related (and other) violence as the increased levels of legal cross-border trade and crossings present opportunities for smuggling and profit. Thus, certain Mexican border cities have become almost synonymous with spectacular and horrific violence, not least Ciudad Juárez, where perhaps over 11,000 people have been killed since January 2007. Although currently experiencing a lull in the rate of killing (in 2012, 797 people were murdered, although we should compare this "success" to the "quiet" year of 2007 when 320 people were killed and Calderón deployed the military and federal police), in 2010 Juárez held the unenviable title of the "World's Most Dangerous City." Based on 2010 census figures, it experienced 240 murders per 100,000 population, or over 3,000 murders total, at a rate of nearly 10 victims a day.[11] In Ciudad Juárez, Nuevo Laredo and smaller towns along the border, the tactics of drug smuggling groups and often unidentified violent actors have included car bombs and improvised explosive devices (IEDs), improvised armoured vehicles, grenades and rocket propelled grenades (RPGs).[12]

---

9. This necessarily brief overview is drawn from Kenny and Serrano, "The Mexican State and Organised Crime", *op. cit.*, pp. 29–53; Kenny and Serrano, "Transition to Dystopia", *op. cit.*, pp. 54–85; and Watt and Zepeda, *op. cit.*

10. Many of Mexico's most infamous drug "kingpins" or *capos* originate from Sinaloa. See Alfredo Corchado, *Midnight in Mexico: A Reporter's Journey through a Country's Descent into Darkness* (New York: The Penguin Press, 2013), p. 38.

11. For an example of the "Most Dangerous City" tag, see Daniel Borunda, "Special Report: 'Juárez Deserves the Title of Most Dangerous City in the World'", *El Paso Times*, 7 June 2010, available: <http://www.elpasotimes.com/juarez/ci_15241689> (accessed 26 July 2013).

12. See William Booth, "Ciudad Juarez Car Bomb Shows New Sophistication in Mexican Drug Cartels' Tactics", *The Washington Post*, 22 July 2010, available: <http://www.washingtonpost.com/wp-dyn/content/article/2010/07/21/AR2010072106200.html> (accessed 26 July 2013); William Booth, "Mexican Cartels Now Using 'Narco Tanks'", *The Washington Post*, 7 June 2011, available: <http://articles.washingtonpost.com/2011-06-07/world/35265552_1_mexican-cartels-drug-cartel-boss-armored-truck> (accessed 26 July 2013); Nick Miroff and William Booth, "Mexican Drug Cartels' Newest Weapon: Cold War-Era Grenades Made in US", *The Washington Post*, 17 July 2010, available: <http://www.washingtonpost.com/wp-dyn/content/article/2010/07/16/AR2010071606252.html?sid=ST2010072106244> (accessed 26 July 2013); Ioan Grillo, "Mexico's Drug Lords Ramp Up Their Arsenals with RPGs", *Time*, 25 October 2012, available:

Perhaps unsurprisingly, the US response to this violence has been in large part connected to a wider frame of "border security" in both official policy and political discourse. In October 2007 the governments of the US and Mexico jointly announced the Mérida Initiative, a wide-ranging $1.4 billion aid package for Mexico that would help Calderón's administration to "break the power and impunity of drug and criminal organizations that threaten the health and public safety of their citizens and the stability and security of the region."[13] While Mérida is broad-based, providing support for variegated Mexican political institutions, it is clear from policy documentation that it was designed with a large border security component, and that this would tie into established programmes and wider strategies, especially those emanating from the focus on homeland security after 9/11. The announcement that greeted the Mérida agreement explicitly connected it to the Southwest Border Counternarcotics Strategy (SBCS), which had been launched earlier in 2007. That strategy emphasised a potential link between counternarcotics (CN), counterterrorism (CT), immigration and homeland security, stating:

> The threat of terrorism looms large wherever criminals regularly exploit gaps in homeland security. Terrorists could conceivably attempt to enter the United States or smuggle weapons of mass destruction (WMD) across the Southwest Border by utilizing routes and methods established by drug and alien smugglers. The US Government's various homeland security missions are interrelated, and, therefore, improved counterdrug efforts will contribute to greater security against other homeland security threats.[14]

Congressional testimony and reporting also confirmed that prior to being legislated, the Mérida Initiative was openly about "Counternarcotics, Counterterrorism and Border Security."[15] Official budgetary justifications outlined that it had "important implications for the Global War on Terror."[16] Policy analysis reveals that much of Mérida was geared towards helping Mexico to secure their side of the border. *Inter alia*, biometric equipment, ion scanners, x-ray vans and software systems to help coordinate cross-border cooperation on security issues has been provided, helping to plug Mexican security forces into the existing US border security framework and the growing convergence of border security issues under the rubric of homeland security in the wake of 9/11.[17]

<http://world.time.com/2012/10/25/mexicos-drug-lords-ramp-up-their-arsenals-with-rpgs/> (accessed 26 July 2013).

13. US Department of State, *Joint Statement on the Mérida Initiative* (Washington, DC, 22 October 2007).

14. US White House Office of National Drug Control Policy, *National Southwest Border Counternarcotics Strategy: Unclassified Summary* (Washington, DC, 2007), p. 2.

15. For example, see the testimony of David T. Johnson, former Assistant Secretary for International Narcotics and Law Enforcement Affairs, in *The Anti-Drug Package for Mexico and Central America: An Evaluation*, Hearing before Senate Committee on Foreign Relations (Serial 110-311), 110th Congress (15 November 2007) and *The Merida Initiative: "Guns, Drugs and Friends"*, Report to the Members of the Senate Committee on Foreign Relations, US Senate, 110th Congress (S. Prt 110-35) (December 2007), pp. 16–26.

16. US Department of State and Agency for International Development, *Supplemental Appropriations Justification Fiscal Year 2008* (Washington, DC, 2008), p. 27.

17. See *Common Enemy, Common Struggle: Progress in US–Mexican Efforts to Defeat Organized Crime and Drug Trafficking*, Report to the Members of the Senate Committee on Foreign Relations, US Senate, 111th Congress (S. Prt 111) (2010), pp. 20–23.

In addition to official policy, there is also a debate about the nature of the threat from Mexico's security crisis and drug trafficking groups to the border region, often pivoting around the existence of "spillover" violence (Mexican drug-related security problems jumping the border) and similar ideas of "threat convergence" as expressed by the SBCS. In 2011 the defence consultancy firm Colgen published a report for the Texas Departments of Public Safety and Agriculture, co-authored by Clinton's former head of the Office of National Drug Control Policy (ONDCP) Barry McCaffrey. It essentially conceptualised the Texan border as a battleground where citizens had to respond to a concerted "narco-terrorist military-style campaign being waged against them."[18] Despite significant evidence that this is an exaggeration,[19] the US media and high profile politicians have also promoted the concept of a violent spillover as a genuine and pervasive phenomenon, intersecting with issues of "illegal immigration" and terrorism.[20] Texan congressman Michael McCaul (R-TX) attempted to introduce legislation that would designate Mexican drug trafficking groups as foreign terrorist organisations on the State Department's (DoS) watch list.[21] Former Florida congressman and defeated 2012 Senate hopeful Connie Mack (R-FL) entered an "Enhanced Border Security Act" bill that would have defined the situation in Mexico as a "terrorist insurgency" while requiring the federal government to produce "a plan to address resources, technology, and infrastructure required to create a secure border area that establishes border security as a top priority of the Government of the United States."[22] The introduced legislation suffered swift congressional death, with significant pushback from federal officials to defining Mexico's *overall* security problem in these terms.[23] Nonetheless, McCaul and Mack were in part responding to congressional testimony from both academics and federal officials that likened

18. Barry R. McCaffrey and Robert H. Scales, "Texas Border Security: A Strategic Military Assessment", Colgen, 20 September 2011, available: <http://www.texasagriculture.gov/Portals/0/DigArticle/1623/46982_Final%20Report-Texas%20Border%20Security.pdf> (accessed 11 August 2014).

19. Undoubtedly some acts of cross-border violence have occurred. See Sylvia Longmire, "Border Violence Spillover: A Growing, but Undefined Problem", *Small Wars Journal*, 15 January 2013, available: <http://smallwarsjournal.com/jrnl/art/border-violence-spillover-a-growing-but-undefined-problem> (accessed 31 July 2013). However, official reports have discussed the difficulty of defining spillover and its limited nature. US GAO, *Southwest Border Security: Data Are Limited and Concerns Vary about Spillover Crime along the Southwest Border* (Washington, DC, February 2013) and Kristin M. Finklea, *Southwest Border Violence: Issues in Identifying and Measuring Spillover Violence* (Congressional Research Service, 2013).

20. Melissa del Boque, "Hyping the New Media Buzzword: 'Spillover' on the Border", *NACLA Report on the Americas* (1 July 2009), available: <https://nacla.org/article/hyping-new-media-buzzword-'spillover'-border> (accessed 11 August 2014).

21. Geoffrey Ramsey, "US Congressman Repeats Call to Designate Mexican Drug Gangs as 'Terrorists'", Insight Crime, 5 October 2011, available: <http://www.insightcrime.org/news-briefs/us-congressman-repeats-calls-to-designate-mexican-drug-gangs-as-terrorists> (accessed 25 May 2013).

22. See HR 3401 (112th Congress): Enhanced Border Security Act (10 November 2011), available: <http://www.govtrack.us/congress/bills/112/hr3401> (accessed 13 May 2013).

23. See the testimony of Assistant Secretary of Bureau of International Narcotics Law Enforcement Affairs (INCLE) William Brownfield, Rodney G. Benson, Assistant Administrator, Chief of Intelligence, Drug Enforcement Administration (DEA) and Mariko Silver, Acting Assistant Secretary, Office of International Affairs, US Department of Homeland Security (DoHS), *Merida Part Two: Insurgency and Terrorism in Mexico*, Hearing before the Subcommittee on the Western Hemisphere of House Committee on Foreign Affairs and Subcommittee on Oversight, Investigations and Management of House Committee on Homeland Security (Serial 112-108/112-48), 112th Congress (4 October 2011), pp. 14, 39–42.

Mexican drug violence to terrorism and insurgency.[24] In one hearing, Assistant Secretary Brownfield conceded to Congressman Mack that "many of the facts on the ground, the things that are being done by those organizations [Mexican drug trafficking groups], are consistent with what we would call either 'terrorism' or 'insurgency' in other countries."[25]

More broadly, former Secretary of State Clinton used the word "insurgency" to describe Mexico's security issues in comparing it to the situation in Colombia in the 1990s, although these were comments her president quickly dismissed.[26] These statements are reflective of wider work within academia and official policy that has sought to explain and define the situation in Mexico as a militarised threat to US national security. Mexico is seen in influential quarters and in policy as a clear case of the national security risk potential posed by the phenomenon broadly defined as TOC—the harmful activities of transnational networks who engage in and facilitate a whole host of illicit activities, running the gamut from money laundering to human trafficking to terrorism.[27] Given the militarised tactics of certain drug trafficking groups (some of which are alluded to above), the invocation of "insurgency" and "national security threat" is at least understandable. Tangentially or otherwise, it also lends discursive and political legitimacy to the agendas of border security advocates, who are able to point to academia and official policy in support of preventing Mexico's security issues from crossing the border.

It is important to establish that Mexico's drug-related security crisis is now firmly enmeshed in a wider and deeper US border security debate and paradigm.[28] However, as we began to see above, this discourse is also afforded serious political space by academic and policy interpretations and responses to the current insecurity in Mexico. Thus, despite significant differences in onus (and of course dissenting voices), official policy, political discourse and academia are further coagulating on the issue of Mexico's security crisis and the border. Alongside debates on immigration and terrorism, this is helping to push a continuing trend towards deeper border

---

24. For example, Mack and McCaul sat on subcommittee meetings where they heard academics Dr. Gary M. Shiffham and Dr. Robert J. Bunker liken Mexican drug trafficking groups to insurgents and "warmaking organizations." See *Has Mérida Evolved: The Evolution of Drug Cartels and the Threat to Mexico's Governance*, Hearing before the Subcommittee on the Western Hemisphere and Subcommittee on Oversight and Investigation of Committee on Foreign Affairs (Serial 110-60), 112th Congress (13 September 2011), pp. 29, 56–57, 62–63.

25. *Emerging Threats and Security in the Western Hemisphere: Next Steps for US Policy*, Hearing before the House Committee on Foreign Affairs (Serial 110-75), 112th Congress (13 October 2011), p. 48.

26. Frank James, "Obama Rejects Hillary Clinton Mexico–Colombia Comparison", *NPR News*, 9 September 2010, available: <http://www.npr.org/blogs/thetwo-way/2010/09/09/129760276/obama-rejects-hillary-clinton-mexico-colombia-comparison> (accessed 3 August 2013).

27. For example, see James G. Stavridis, "Foreword", in Miklaucic and Brewer, *Convergence*, *op. cit.*, pp. vii–x. Stavridis is former US Southern Command (USSOUTHCOM) and European Command (USEUCOM) Commander and the former Supreme Allied Commander for Europe in the North Atlantic Treaty Organisation (NATO); Martin Edward Andersen, "A Roadmap for Beating Latin America's Transnational Criminal Organizations", *Joint Forces Quarterly*, Vol. 62 (July 2011), pp. 81–88; Robert Killebrew, "Criminal Insurgency in the Americas and Beyond", *NDU Prism*, Vol. 2, No. 3 (June 2011), pp. 33–52; Council on Foreign Relations, "Symposium on Organized Crime in the Western Hemisphere: An Overlooked Threat?", 18 November 2009, available: <http://www.cfr.org/transnational-crime/session-one-council-foreign-relations-symposium-organized-crime-western-hemisphere-overlooked-threat/p20823> (accessed 14 July 2013); US White House: National Security Council, *The Strategy to Combat Transnational Organized Crime* (Washington, DC, 2010).

28. Mathew Coleman, "US Statecraft and the US–Mexico Border as Security/Economy Nexus", *Political Geography*, Vol. 24 (2005), pp. 192–194.

security and seemingly "harder" borders, whether intentionally or otherwise. The immigration reform bill that passed the Senate on 27 June 2013 required an extensive amendment that added $38 billion in border security spending to even be able to convince enough members to vote for it.[29] The final bill, if enacted (which is doubtful at the time of writing), would "appropriate $46.3 billion for expenses related to the security of the southern US border and initial administrative costs."[30] Thus, we can conclude that Mexico's security crisis is part of the increasing US focus on border security. This means that US CN policy at the border is plugged into the heart of a growing problem for US policymakers: the border paradox.

The Border Paradox

The Ties that Bind: US–Mexico Economic Relations

The basis of the border paradox is quite simple. As border security has become more of an issue for the US, the importance to the US of its economic relationship with Mexico, which is rooted in greatly increased cross-border exchange, has deepened. Essentially, there appear to be two trends clashing with regard to the US–Mexico relationship: greater economic integration and mutual importance, and a greater focus on security at the south-west border. To understand this, it is key to establish the growing importance of US–Mexican economic ties, which have deepened alongside the increased border security policy and rhetoric outlined above. This economic relationship has always been a significant one, notably in areas such as factory production,[31] "flexible" labour importation[32] and energy.[33] However, the passage of NAFTA in 1994 has in many ways rendered Mexico crucial to contemporary US economic success (and, albeit in a different and more profound manner, vice versa).

Mexico was the US's third largest trading partner in 2012 behind fellow NAFTA member Canada and (with far higher imports but lower exports) China.[34] Overall bilateral trade is currently hovering around $500 billion in goods and services,

29. Alexander Bolton and Justin Sink, "Senate Immigration Bill Gets Major Boost with Border Security Agreement", *The Hill*, 20 June 2013, available: <http://thehill.com/blogs/blog-briefing-room/news/306739-reports-senators-reach-tentative-deal-on-border-security-> (accessed 17 July 2013). For figures, see US Congressional Budget Office, "Letter to Senator Patrick Leahy Impact of Senate Amendment 1183 to Bill S. 744" (Washington, DC, 24 June 2013), p. 2.

30. S. 744 (113th Congress), *Border Security, Economic Opportunity, and Immigration Modernization Act* (16 April 2013), p. 11.

31. The *maquiladora* cross-border factory initiative was started in 1965, partially in response to the end of the Bracero programme that had allowed Mexican workers temporary work visas in the US.

32. Through various official and unofficial means, including the aforementioned Bracero programme, which ran from 1943 to 1964, Mexican workers have made up a shortfall of labour in the US, especially in the agriculture and service industries. This has also provided a valve for Mexican unemployment pressures.

33. Through the 1980s and 1990s Mexican crude oil exports to the US rose and it is now consistently a top-three exporter to the US market. Despite declining production and exploration difficulties that have resulted in falling exports since 2004, 972,000 barrels per day arrived from Mexico in 2012, around 11.5 per cent of total US crude imports. See US Energy Information Administration, *Mexico: Country Analysis*, available: <http://www.eia.gov/countries/cab.cfm?fips=MX>; and *Petroleum and Other Liquids: Data: Crude Oil: US Imports by Country of Origin*, available: <http://www.eia.gov/dnav/pet/pet_move_impcus_a2_nus_epc0_im0_mbblpd_a.htm> (accessed 30 June 2013).

34. United States Census Bureau, *Trade in Goods with Mexico*, available: <http://www.census.gov/foreign-trade/balance/c2010.html#1993> (accessed 20 May 2013).

which represents a total trade increase of over 500 per cent between 1993 and 2012.[35] Much of this trade of course is accounted for by *maquiladora* processing plants, export assembly businesses that receive duty-free US components for much cheaper assembly by Mexican labour, with final products exported back into the US at comparatively lower tariffs. Although the *maquila* programme was started in the 1960s, it received a huge boost through NAFTA, and between 1970 and 2006 the number of plants operating in Mexico increased from 120 to 2,810.[36] Despite experiencing significant economic pressures from an increasingly competitive China in the 21st century, and shocks from the downturn associated with the financial crisis in 2007–2009, several large border complexes integral to the North American supply chain now exist, such as El Paso–Ciudad Juárez and San Diego–Tijuana (and their immediately surrounding areas). These hubs are not based only around trade, but also cross-border production and transportation elsewhere in several key industries. Looking at the El Paso–Ciudad Juárez region gives us some more insight here. In 2012 almost 725,000 trucks and over 33,000 loaded rail containers crossed the border at El Paso Points of Entry (POEs) alone.[37] Over $65 billion in transborder freight moved through El Paso–Ciudad Juárez in 2012, including $43 billion in trade groups that include parts and components for assembly in the *maquilas* and factories that straddle the two major cities and surrounding areas.[38] Furthermore, cross-border economic impacts are not limited to trade figures. Almost 10 million cars crossed the border alongside over six million pedestrians,[39] generating and sustaining a cross-border retail economy and reflecting a cross-border lifestyle in terms of work, family life and leisure.[40]

In addition, Mexico has become increasingly important for North American competiveness, albeit within more globalised economic processes and trends, and that has large implications for the US's global economic success. Across the NAFTA zone, "just in time" production (whereby the smaller components of a larger product are delivered "just in time" for final assembly, giving greater flexibility for customers and saving on inventory costs and problems),[41] use of labour "flexibility" (advantageous wage differentials) and innovative tariff arrangements have

35. M. Angles Villareal and Ian F. Ferguson, *NAFTA at 20: Overview and Trade Effects* (Congressional Research Service, 2013), p. 10.

36. César M. Fuentes and Sergio Peña, "Globalization, Transborder Networks, and US–Mexico Border Cities", in Kathleen Staudt, César M. Fuentes and Julia E. Monárrez Fragoso (eds.), *Cities and Citizenship at the US–Mexico Border: The Paso del Norte Metropolitan Region* (New York: Palgrave Macmillan, 2010), p. 10.

37. United States Department of Transportation: Research and Innovative Technology Administration Bureau of Transportation Statistics, "Border Crossing Entry Data: El Paso 2012", available: <http://transborder.bts.gov/programs/international/transborder/TBDR_BC/TBDR_BCQ.html> (accessed 30 July 2013).

38. United States Department of Transportation: Research and Innovative Technology Administration Bureau of Transportation Statistics, "North American Transborder Freight Data: Port and Commodity Data El Paso 2012", available: <http://transborder.bts.gov/programs/international/transborder/TBDR_QAPC07.html> (accessed 30 July 2013).

39. Department of Transportation "Border Crossing Entry Data", *op. cit.*

40. See, for example, Tony Payan, *The Three US–Mexico Border Wars: Drugs, Immigration, and Homeland Security* (Westport, CT: Praeger Security International, 2006), pp. 2–3, 5.

41. For a discussion of the "just in time" process in the auto industry, see Thomas Klier and James Rubenstein, *Who Really Made Your Car? Restructuring and Geographic Change in the Auto Industry* (Kalamazoo, MI: Upjohn Institute for Employment Research, 2008), pp. 135–141.

revolutionised areas of North American production. This is responsible for a significant chunk of the increase in North American trade, both in the parts traded for assembly in cross-border *maquila* plants and factories, and in final products.[42] Looking at figures for trade gives us an insight into this phenomenon, as some of the top items (outside oil and associated products) are similar for both imports and exports, including electronic equipment (parts and products) and auto (parts and products).[43] For example, "American" automotive manufacture can now be increasingly said to be "North American," given the integral role that Mexico and Canada play in the truly trilateral production process (although the US retail market retains dominance).[44]

Beyond this trend, several key economic areas for US interests exist. Mexico remains a key agricultural trading partner (although given the huge subsidies that allow overproducing US farms to use Mexico as an uncompetitive market, the concept of "partnership" may be stretched here). Nonetheless, Mexico has steadily increased its exports to the US at a rate of almost 10 per cent year on year since NAFTA, albeit through the decline of small-scale farming and the increased dominance of agribusiness.[45] Mexico also remains an important supplier of raw materials to the US and global markets, but while Mexico's trade portfolio in goods remains heavily made up by oil and associated products (14 per cent of exports and 9 per cent of imports in 2012), and Mexico is a major source of other key resources (notably silver and gold), in terms of percentages products tied to bi-national and North American assembly processes (and the subsequent final products) dominate US–Mexican trade. Thus, the argument that Delgado-Ramos and María Romano make suggesting that Mexico is important to the US as chiefly a raw materials exporter is rather outdated. Its political economic importance now goes far beyond that.[46]

We can also see this in energy production and security, itself also increasingly "North American." While Mexico's crude oil exports to the US currently retain their importance, the US supplied Mexico with over 82 per cent of non-crude refined petroleum products in 2012, and is set to take advantage of its shale gas boom by partnering with Petróleos Mexicanos (PEMEX) in creating pipelines that will stretch across the border and deep into Mexico's territory.[47] Mexico has very large deposits of technically recoverable shale gas in deposits in the east

42. Shannon K. O'Neil, *Two Nations Indivisible: Mexico, the United States, and the Road Ahead* (Oxford: Oxford University Press, 2013), pp. 113–116; Robert A. Pastor, *The North American Idea: A Vision of a Continental Future* (Oxford: Oxford University Press, 2011), pp. 100–101.

43. See International Trade Centre, "Trade Map: Mexico & United States", available: <http://www.trademap.org/countrymap/Bilateral_TS.aspx> (accessed 22 July 2013).

44. Krista Hughes, "Mexican Manufacturing: From Sweatshops to High-Tech Motors", Reuters, 9 April 2013, available: <http://www.reuters.com/article/2013/04/09/us-mexico-economy-manufacturing-idUSBRE9380TN20130409> (accessed 9 May 2013); Thomas H. Klier and James M. Rubenstein, "The Growing Importance of Mexico in North America's Auto Production", The Federal Reserve Bank of Chicago, Chicago Fed Letter No. 310 (May 2013).

45. For trade figures, see US Department of Agriculture, *Strengthening NAFTA through US–Mexican Cooperation in Agriculture* (Washington, DC, March 2007), p. 2.

46. Gian Carlo Delgado-Ramos and Silvina María Romano, "Political-Economic Factors in US Foreign Policy: The Colombia Plan, the Mérida Initiative, and the Obama Administration", *Latin American Perspectives*, Vol. 38, No. 4 (2011), pp. 101–103. Trade figures from International Trade Centre, *op. cit.*

47. "Mexico's Pemex Opens Contract Bids for Ramones Gas Pipeline Project", Reuters, 13 May 2013, available: <http://www.reuters.com/article/2013/05/13/mexico-gas-idUSL2N0DU2KR20130513> (accessed 14 May 2013).

and especially the north-east of its territory, a very tempting resource for large foreign investment and potentially an important contributor to North American energy security (although the violence in this region may be a consideration for investors, of which more below). In February 2012 the two countries signed a Transboundary Hydrocarbons Agreement, designed to provide a mutual framework for deep sea oil reserves in the Gulf of Mexico under previously unclear national jurisdiction. The DoS touted that the agreement could lead to (albeit limited) joint ventures between US firms and PEMEX, and that it provided legal certainty for potential investment in exploratory drilling.[48] At the time of the agreement, US officials hoped it would help to galvanise the push by Calderón's government to open up the oil sector to foreign private investment and expertise that could help boost ailing production.[49] The depletion of Mexico's oil reserves, especially at the huge Cantarell oil field,[50] and PEMEX's lack of experience in deep water drilling has potentially significant implications for the US and wider North American energy security, given that 11.5 per cent of US crude imports in 2012 came from Mexico. The impact on Mexico's overall political economic stability also concerned the US, according to diplomatic cables, given the huge input PEMEX provides to Mexico's federal and therefore national budgets.[51] US officials concluded that if negotiations for a transboundary agreement "promote a future opening of the Mexican oil sector to foreign participation, it would be a positive development for all involved."[52] Peña Nieto's administration has finally pushed through reforms along these lines. Should they meet the hopes of several commentators,[53] and Mexico's oil production opens up successfully to private investment, energy integration is likely to go further.[54] Mexico's importance to the US is underlined in these energy issues.

48. US Department of State, *Fact Sheet: US–Mexico Transboundary Hydrocarbons Agreement* (Washington, DC, 2 May 2013).

49. According to a WikiLeaks cable, International Oil Companies (IOCs) didn't think any transboundary reserves would be of great significance in size, and US officials speculated that the Mexican government pushed the issue as part of its attempts to reform the energy sector and open it up. US Embassy Mexico, *Transboundary Reservoirs—What is Motivating Mexico?*, Cable Reference 00000635 (3 March 2009), available: <http://www.cablegatesearch.net/cable.php?id=09MEXICO635> (accessed 6 August 2013).

50. See Michael T. Klare, *The Race for What's Left: The Global Scramble for the World's Last Resources* (New York: Picador, 2012), pp. 19–22.

51. US Embassy Mexico, *Economic Conditions in Mexico*, Cable Reference 000033 (7 January 2009), available: <http://www.cablegatesearch.net/cable.php?id=09MEXICO33&q=china%20mexico> (accessed 13 October 2012).

52. US Embassy Mexico, *Transboundary Reservoirs*, *op. cit.*

53. For example, *The Economist*, "Choose Pemex Over the Pact", 13 July 2013, available: <http://www.economist.com/news/leaders/21581730-successful-cross-party-pact-has-broken-congressional-gridlock-it-must-not-become-obstacle> (accessed 13 July 2013); Nick Snow, "Mexico Reforms Seen as Key to North American Energy Alliance", *Oil and Gas Journal*, 24 July 2013, available: <http://www.ogj.com/articles/2013/07/mexico-reforms-seen-as-key-to-north-american-energy-alliance.html> (accessed 3 August 2013); Russell Crandall, "Mexico's Domestic Economy: Policy Options and Choices", in Russell Crandall, Guadalupe Paz and Riordan Roett (eds.), *Mexico's Democracy at Work: Political and Economic Dynamics* (Boulder, CO: Lynne Rienner Publishers, 2005), pp. 81–82; Pastor, *op. cit.*, pp. 104, 159.

54. However, lest we think North American energy integration is a simple linear process, the proposed controversial Keystone XL project, which represents deeper bilateral integration with Canada, has the potential to undercut Mexico's crude exports. Paul W. Parfomak, Robert Pirog, Linda Luther and Adam Vann, *Keystone XL Pipeline Project: Key Issues* (Congressional Research Service, 2013), pp. 23–24.

Finally, on a more macro-policy level, both Mexico and Canada are now negotiating members of the Trans-Pacific Partnership (TPP), a key component of the US strategic "rebalance" towards Asia, and this is in itself undoubtedly a potential catalyst for ever more integration across these areas and possibly in new areas.[55] The cumulative effect of these important developments is not just the result of blind processes of globalisation, but also sustained policy. US and receptive Mexican policymakers encouraged the opening up of Mexico's relatively closed economy to integration and investment following Mexico's huge economic crash(es) from 1982 onwards. NAFTA was the culmination of US strategic-economic policy towards Mexico, whereby the country became a testing ground for conditional aid through the International Monetary Fund (IMF) and World Bank (WB), given in return for deep economic restructuring based on market liberalisation, privatisation and economic openness. As Ikenberry points out, NAFTA was a way for both US policymakers and the Salinas technocrats to "lock in the commitments" to trade and market liberalisation that had been undertaken in the previous decade.[56]

The Border Paradox: Economy and Security Trade Offs?

We saw how Mexico's security crisis had been pulled into a wider trend of hardening rhetoric on the US–Mexico border. The rhetoric is also documented physically in the increase in active border patrol agents (increasing from 3,444 agents in Fiscal Year [FY] 1993 to over 18,000 in FY 2012)[57] and wider increasing visibility of US Customs and Border Protection (CBP),[58] the implementation of aggressive and deliberately public deterrence initiatives such as Operation "Hold the Line" in El Paso, and Operation Gatekeeper in San Diego,[59] the growing use of surveillance and inspection equipment and the construction of imposing (but by no means impenetrable) fences along several sections of the border. These various programmes and trends have been given added impetus by the events of 9/11, and are now ostensibly organised under the rubric of homeland security. However, the border paradox begins to kick in as we consider that the efforts to increase border or homeland security appear to have had a tangible economic cost. Security inspections by customs or border patrol officers and agents[60] take time, and that impacts trade, especially with regard to the just in time processes and agricultural

55. For background here see Ian F. Fergusson, William H. Cooper, Remy Jurenas and Brock R. Williams, *The Trans-Pacific Partnership Negotiations and Issues for Congress* (Congressional Research Service, 2013); Hillary Clinton, "America's Pacific Century", *Foreign Policy* (November 2011), available: <http://www.foreignpolicy.com/articles/2011/10/11/americas_pacific_century> (accessed 22 July 2013).

56. See G. John Ikenberry, *After Victory: Institutions, Strategic Restraint, and the Rebuilding of Order after Major Wars* (Princeton, NJ: Princeton University Press, 2000), pp. 239–242.

57. US Department of Homeland Security: Customs and Border Protection, *Border Patrol Agent Staffing by Fiscal Year*, available: <http://www.cbp.gov/sites/default/files/documents/U.S.%20Border%20Patrol%20Fiscal%20Year%20Staffing%20Statistics%201992-2013.pdf> (accessed 11 August 2014). The current Senate bill for immigration reform proposes to double these numbers again.

58. For increases in CBP budgets and personnel in apparent response to drug trafficking and terrorism fears, see Andreas, *Border Games*, *op. cit.*, pp. 55, 154.

59. Timothy J. Dunn, *Blockading the Border and Human Rights: The El Paso Operation that Remade Immigration Enforcement* (Austin, TX: University of Texas Press, 2009); Joseph Nevins, *Operation Gatekeeper: The War on "Illegals" and the Remaking of the US–Mexico Boundary* (2nd edition) (New York: Routledge, 2010).

60. Customs officers operate at points of entry themselves. Border patrol agents, as part of their overall strategy, run inspection checkpoints set back from the border on major highways and roads.

traffic so key to North American production, consumption and competitiveness. O'Neil cites a Chamber of Commerce report that claims the US economy loses $6 billion in output and 26,000 jobs annually with 2008 wait times.[61] Although the justification for these high numbers is thin,[62] the U.S. Government Accountability Office (GAO) used more circumspect studies and removed "multiplier effects" to posit still serious direct impacts of wait times at regional and national levels.[63]

Beyond attempts to accurately chart the precise adverse economic effects of a hardened border, there is plenty of wider (perhaps commonsensical) evidence to support this phenomenon, from the decline in legal border crossings to the conclusions of regional and national leaders and officials, the costs imposed on businesses and so on.[64] Thus, border analysts and scholars of US–Mexican relations have seen two competing trends in the US–Mexico relationship and the wider NAFTA region: increased economic integration through heightened reciprocal (albeit uneven) important economic interaction, and a greater focus, at least from the US side, on border security. Here, then, is one version of the border paradox: the tension between integration and security that seemingly manifests itself at the border. Pastor summarises this succinctly: "two countervailing pressures—to create a seamless market or to construct barriers to impede transit—have led to a North America that is stuck between two worlds."[65]

However, there are different conclusions on the reasons behind this phenomenon, and its import. For some, including Pastor, much of the fact that it even exists can be blamed on misguided or careless US policy. Pastor sees the prevalence of the border security paradigm—encouraged by the sort of domestic US politics we glimpsed above, catalysed to new levels by the 9/11 attacks, institutionalised in the Department for Homeland Security and now, as we have seen, incorporating reactions to Mexico's drug-related security crisis—as a profoundly dysfunctional and counterproductive development. He contends that it has been an effective wrench in the gears of continued North American integration, economic expansion and success, and that effectively the border security "pressure" is currently trumping the (more desirable) pressure of economic integration.[66] Bailey and Guillén-Lopéz to a degree concur, arguing that "most of the attention to the border has been driven by US conceptions of security."[67] Others have also emphasised the role of policy in creating efficiency problems at the border and stifling the economic potential of US–Mexican integration. Within these accounts there is often an

61. O'Neil, *Two Nations*, *op. cit.*, p. 119.

62. For example, it appears the report commits an error that the GAO has identified in assuming an unrealistic "no wait" scenario and thus designating every minute a truck is "in line"—from entering the inspection lane in Mexico until passing US inspection—as a delay. US Department of Commerce, *Improving Economic Outcomes by Reducing Border Delays* (Washington, DC, 2008), p. 8.

63. US GAO, *US–Mexico Border: CBP Action Needed to Improve Wait Time Data and Measure Outcomes of Trade Facilitation Efforts* (Washington, DC, 2013), pp. 44–50.

64. For a good overview of some of this evidence, see Pastor, *op. cit.*, pp. 116–127. Also see Erik Lee and Christopher Wilson, *The State of Trade, Competitiveness and Economic Well-being in the US–Mexico Border Region* (Pennsylvania: Woodrow Wilson Center, Mexico Institute, June 2012), p. 9.

65. Pastor, *op. cit.*, p. 110.

66. This is paraphrasing a quote by former US ambassador to Canada Paul Celluci to the effect that after 9/11, "security trumps trade." *Ibid.*, p. 114.

67. John Bailey and Tonatiuh Guillén-Lopéz, "Making and Managing Policy", in Smith and Selee, *Mexico and the United States*, *op. cit.*, p. 77. These two authors do look seriously at the Security and Prosperity Partnership, a stalled trilateral effort announced in 2005 to push forward both the NAFTA agenda and a trilateral security framework for the region, but conclude that it largely failed.

implicit or explicit exhortation to recalibrate US border policy from one focused on security towards one that hones in on the economic potential that could be unleashed through an effective, trade-facilitating border. This is not to say that these analysts do not consider border security a policy priority, but that it is one that is currently overstated, led by sectional interest groups or political factions and counterproductive or even a failure on its own terms. For example, O'Neil suggests that increased spending on border infrastructure at POEs (rather than perhaps a focus on the gaps between them manned by border patrol) would "help the United States achieve two goals at the same time; allowing in the good trade, and keeping out the bad."[68]

Meanwhile, Wilson and Lee advocate the increased use of technology and border security programmes like SENTRI, FAST and C-TAPT, respectively the Secure Electronic Network for Travelers Rapid Inspection (trusted traveller permits for pedestrians and "civilian" vehicles on the US–Mexico border), Free and Secure Trade (for commercial truck drivers in the NAFTA zone) and Customs-Trade Partnership against Terrorism (global public-private programme whereby trusted companies agree to improve security processes in exchange for expedited inspection). They describe these initiatives as a "win-win-win" in that they would encourage faster, more productive trade while simultaneously being economical and helping to improve border security.[69] All of these accounts also encourage greater partnership with Mexico under agreements like the Mérida Initiative, and even suggest that the US should, "reduce [...] efforts to fortify the border."[70] Thus, in this reading, the border paradox is in fact not so much a paradox as a policy challenge that US policymakers are thus far failing to meet, mainly because they have not paid enough attention to the *economic* reality of the border in favour of misguided or ideological fixations on security.

However, this reading severely underplays the complexity of the paradox, as recognised by other authors. After the attacks of 9/11,[71] Andreas has noted the negative economic impact of an increased focus on border security and more thorough border security measures, stating that, "[a]s a result of the post-September 11 border enforcement crackdown, security has become a new kind of trade barrier."[72] In response to this, he sees border security increasing in a "policed" manner, whereby the goals of the state are to deny access to clandestine transnational actors (or, in his terminology, "CTAs")—traffickers, immigrants and terrorists—while simultaneously facilitating the flow of legitimate commerce and trade.[73] Generally speaking, creating a border closed in some respects and open in others is inherently difficult. Serrano suggests that the challenge of NAFTA's "new security environment"—marked by licit and illicit transnational flows and

68. O'Neil, *Two Nations, op cit.*, p. 120. Also see Erik Lee and Erik L. Olsen, "The State of Security in the US–Mexico Border Region", in Christopher L. Wilson and Erik Lee, *The State of the Border Report: A Comprehensive Analysis of the US–Mexico Border* (Pennsylvania: Woodrow Wilson Center, Mexico Institute, May 2013), p. 91.

69. Lee and Wilson, *op. cit.*, p. 13.

70. Peter H. Smith and Andrew Selee, "Prospects for Partnership", in Smith and Selee, *Mexico and the United States, op. cit.*, p. 199.

71. Andreas had previously argued that in fact with regard to the border security paradigm *prior to 9/11*, it was *economics that trumped security.*

72. Peter Andreas, "Redrawing the Line: Borders and Security in the 21st Century", *International Security*, Vol. 28, No. 2 (2003), p. 93.

73. *Ibid.*, pp. 95–96.

a "putative new species of terrorism"—overwhelmed border security and "opened a serious gap between what these border measures were designed to achieve and what they are now expected to deliver."[74] Gilbert states on a macro-level that North American integration is therefore marked by "fragmented and *contradictory* security interests" and that there exist "simultaneous pressures to more forcefully delineate national territoriality *and* to deepen North American integration."[75] We should understand this dialectic between integration and security in the NAFTA zone as a unique, regional example of a wider phenomenon: the increase in the "scope, reach, and intensity" of illicit activity and economy within the concomitant increases in economic flows and interconnectedness in globalisation,[76] and the tension-riddled response of many states in trying to block or control the illicit flows (including "illegal" migration) while facilitating the licit ones.

The challenge for US policymakers has become "how to forge a sustainable common security outlook against the new security threat [specifically terrorism, though we may add wider border security concerns] without sacrificing advantages of economic integration?"[77] President Bush summarised the dilemma and the desired US response rather succinctly when, in the aftermath of 9/11, he told former head of customs Robert Bonner, "You've got to secure our borders against the terrorist threat. But you have to do it without shutting down the US economy."[78] Of course, the "terrorist threat" can be understood more widely in this specific US–Mexican context given the conflation of drugs and immigration issues with terrorism under a wider rubric of US state surveillance and control, whatever the veracity of such links (an issue we return to below). Policymakers are therefore well aware of this dilemma, and the various official references to the twin goals of trade facilitation and security. The DoHS's policy of "risk management," the concept of "smart borders" and the use of some of the more technological solutions introduced earlier in the discussion are testament to the US's attempt to "square the circle" at the border.[79] Nonetheless, the depth of the border paradox ensures that Bush's edict has proved easier said than done for several reasons.

First of all, advances in border security technology, infrastructure and processes (such as C-TAPT), for example, will help trade facilitation. They may also have an improved deterrent effect alongside improved interdiction levels with regards to drugs, potential terrorists, illegal immigration and so on. However, there will be an economic impact to any inspection regime, and security gains will be limited

---

74. Monica Serrano, "Integration and Security in North America: Do Good Neighbours Need Good Fences?", *International Journal*, Vol. 61, No. 3 (2006), p. 621.

75. Emily Gilbert, "Borders and Security in North America", in Jeffrey Ayres and Laura Macdonald (eds.), *North America in Question: Regional Integration in an Era of Economic Turbulence* (Toronto: University of Toronto Press, 2012), p. 197, emphasis added.

76. Richard Friman and Peter Andreas, "Introduction", in Friman and Andreas, *The Illicit Global Economy, op. cit.*, pp. 1–23.

77. Imtiaz Hussain, Satya R. Pattnayak and Anil Hira, *North American Homeland Security: Back to Bilateralism* (Westport, CT: Praeger Security International, 2008), p. 3.

78. Edward Alden, *The Closing of the American Border: Terrorism, Immigration, and Security since 9/11* (New York: Harper Perennial, 2008), p. 52.

79. The 21st Century Border Management programme summarises these goals in making the border both "efficient and secure." US State Department Bureau of Western Hemisphere Affairs, *United States–Mexico Partnership: Managing our 21st Century Border: Fact Sheet* (Washington, DC, 30 April 2013). On the DoHS risk management approach, see US Department of Homeland Security, *Risk Management Fundamentals: Homeland Security Risk Management Doctrine* (Washington, DC, April 2011).

in terms of an "overall" consideration.[80] Aside from problems of trust and corruption inherent in any human activity, the sheer density of trade, which we saw in broad strokes above, precludes anything even approaching absolute security being achievable at the border. Andreas quotes a US Customs Service official speaking in 1996 who claimed that sufficiently rigorous border inspections of trucks for *just* narcotics at the US–Mexico POEs would lead to a situation whereby vehicles were backed up to Mexico City within two weeks.[81] While hard to verify, this presents a vivid picture of potential chaos that would only be deeper with today's trade levels. In any case, the huge economic costs incurred as enhanced security measures were enforced immediately following 9/11 gave all three NAFTA countries a real taste of what such security vigilance would look like, and the costs it would impose on North American business.[82] Additionally, recent revelations regarding Wachovia and HSBC's money laundering protections being thoroughly compromised by drug profit laundering operations emanating from Mexico affirm that borders are not just physical, and that licit and illicit financial flows are deeply intertwined.[83] Better enforcement on laundering is extremely challenging considering that US officials have argued that criminally prosecuting such an integral economic institution as HSBC could have "collateral consequences" that render it inconceivable.[84] Smarter borders and technology may help here, but are not a panacea.

Secondly, there are two interrelated negative feedback loops that operate within North American economic integration and the enhancement of border security programmes and institutions. On a more prosaic level, Andreas has argued convincingly that each round of border security that fails to *achieve* border security provides opportunities for politicians to demand more funding and personnel, bureaucracies to expand their budgets and remits, and leaders and policymakers to gain more perception-related gains.[85] More perniciously, however, further security initiatives are also required because both border security itself and economic openness help to generate the very problems border security is supposed to address. Thus, in Darwinian fashion,[86] increasing border surveillance increases border problems by honing the expertise and raising the profit margins of drug traffickers, immigration *coyotes* and other illicit actors. Moreover, these actors operate within and are empowered by the very economic integration that has

80. On the limits of technology to improve border processes, see Coleman, *op. cit.*, p. 199.

81. Andreas, *Border Games*, *op. cit.*, p. 76.

82. For example, Alden, *op. cit.*, pp. 41–48; Isidro Morales, *Post NAFTA North America: Reshaping the Political and Economic Governance of a Changing Region* (New York: Palgrave Macmillan, 2008), p. 148.

83. Ed Vulliamy, "How a Big US Bank Laundered Billions from Mexico's Murderous Drug Gangs", *Observer*, 2 April 2011, available: <http://www.theguardian.com/world/2011/apr/03/us-bank-mexico-drug-gangs> (accessed 3 August 2013); *US Vulnerabilities to Money Laundering, Drugs, and Terrorist Financing: HSBC Case History*, Report from the Senate Committee on Homeland Security and Governmental Affairs Permanent Subcommittee on Investigations, US Senate, 112th Congress (17 July 2012).

84. Dominic Rushe and Jill Treanor, "HSBC's Record $1.9bn Fine Preferable to Prosecution, US Authorities Insist", *Guardian*, 11 December 2012, available: <http://www.theguardian.com/business/2012/dec/11/hsbc-fine-prosecution-money-laundering?guni=Article:in%20body%20link> (accessed 2 August 2013).

85. Andreas, *Border Games*, *op. cit.*, pp. 11–12.

86. For a brief but sound argument about how US CN policy acts as artificial selection, creating more and more efficient and ruthless traffickers, see Sanho Tree, "What Darwin Teaches about the Drug War", *Common Dreams*, 27 December 2007, available: <https://www.commondreams.org/archive/2007/12/27/6018> (accessed 14 August 2013).

been created and developed between the US and Mexico, through the increasing use of commercial and trade networks that the US has sought to establish in the NAFTA zone. The sheer magnitude of border trade, and the increase in cross-border socioeconomic connections, in many senses officially desired and lauded developments, provide symbiotically increased opportunities for smuggling, and less and less hope of fully policing it.[87]

Thus, the border paradox *is* truly paradoxical as it is sustained not only by the negative impacts security regimes have on trade and wider economic interaction, but also the inseparable licit/illicit economy, the border security feedback loops and the perverse outcomes that result from their interaction. While scholars such as Pastor and O'Neil have noted the clash between security concerns and deeper integration and facilitated trade, and that traffickers have taken advantage of increased border trade to increase profits,[88] they have tended to underplay the fact that many of the challenges to border security have been significantly enhanced and sustained by economic integration. Economic integration feeds some of the challenges that undermine it, and these tensions manifest themselves at the border. However, we still need to briefly establish a more complete picture as to why this is becoming such a policy problem for the US. I understand this differently to the analysts covered here, in that I focus on the nature of US interests.

Why the Paradox? Mexican Security and US Interests

To truly understand the border paradox, it is important that we develop a clearer conceptual understanding of US interests in the NAFTA context, and the threats to those interests. To do this, we need to outline the simple but fundamental point that economic and security interests are not distinct, but profoundly bounded up together. We have seen that those who seek to promote the economic integration of NAFTA have bemoaned the new and harmful focus on security. Clearly, a distinction between security and economic interests is being made here. However, those analysts who helped reveal that the border paradox ran deeper than this also reinforce that distinction. For Andreas, "the imperatives of security and economic integration appear to be on a collision course."[89] The impact of 9/11 is crucial here. Díez is quite typical of border academia in assessing that after the attacks the US subordinated "economic and political relations" with its NAFTA partners to its own security needs, including increased border control and surveillance, in the context of the War on Terror.[90] Serrano speculates as to whether security would provide the integrative dynamo for North America that was initially provided by economics in the designs for NAFTA.[91] While these distinctions may at times be in the service of conceptual clarity, they give an impression of interests neatly

87. See Andreas, *Border Games*, *op. cit.*, pp. 74–82; Friman and Andreas, "Introduction", *op. cit.*, pp. 12–13; Peter Andreas, "When Policies Collide: Market Reform, Market Prohibition, and the Narcotization of the Mexican Economy", in Friman and Andreas, *The Illicit Global Economy*, *op. cit.*, pp. 125–141.

88. For example, see O'Neil, *Two Nations*, *op. cit.*, p. 120 and Shannon K. O'Neil, "The Real War in Mexico: How Democracy can Defeat the Drug Cartels", *Foreign Affairs* (July/August 2009), p.65, where it is pointed out that both Mexico's democratic upheaval and its increased economic integration with the US are factors in the increased power of drug traffickers.

89. Andreas, "A Tale of Two Borders", *op. cit.*, p. 19.

90. Jordi Díez, "Mexico and North American Security", in Daniel Drache (ed.), *Big Picture Realities: Canada and Mexico at the Crossroads* (Ontario: Wilfred Laurier University Press, 2008), pp. 153–168.

91. Serrano, *op. cit.*, p. 626.

compartmentalised as discrete, differentiated aims. This denudes the crucial fused nature of economic-security interests.

A thorough delineation of what constitutes "interests" and how they "work" as motivating forces in foreign policy is beyond the scope of this article. However, some basic points can be laid down here in support of their co-formative essence. As International Relations realists note (albeit with distinct theoretical flourishes), economic success is crucial to continued state or national security in its role in providing the means to defend oneself, or project one's power. However, accepting this necessarily implies the inverse, whereby economic interests can also generate security concerns and needs. We can perhaps bring both security and economic interests together, therefore, as *strategic* interests. This is of course a well-established argument. I draw on Layne here as an exemplar and basis. In revisiting Appleman Williams' "Open Door" thesis of US foreign policy, Layne has identified how US economic expansion and investment through the Open Door created "new interests abroad" that require protection. Therefore, economic interests of the kind we have outlined here with regard to Mexico have "pulled US military power along in its wake."[92] However, this process is more structural than Layne allows, in the sense that these are *core* interests for the US. Layne tends to critique the expansionist tendency inherent in this process as ideational at root, and indeed misguided.[93] To reiterate, we should understand them as strategic, as failing to ensure them would have real implications and costs for US success and security.

Of course, Layne is referring to foreign policy or grand strategy. In the NAFTA context, due to the creation of a regional North American economic (and thereby strategic) space, things are, in an important manner, more complex. Thus, although US interests in Mexico and its wider immediate region pre-date (and indeed informed) NAFTA, the creation of a North American space through that trade agreement and wider economic trends has generated a deeper imperative for the US in securing that space from real and potential threats. This produces regional connections between US homeland security and security in Mexico (and Canada) that are deeper than US strategic interests elsewhere. The levels of trade and productive integration in North America have made the NAFTA zone key to US economic competitiveness, energy security and the US's wider global strategic goals. The brute fact of neighbourliness offers both advantages and complications in this context. Returning to the impact of 9/11, those analysts who bemoan the economic impact of harder borders after 9/11, or posit that security interests have trumped or clash with economic ones, underplay the fact that the US policy response is in large part about ensuring that such attacks do not threaten strategic US interests in the North American economic space.

The events of 9/11 brutally highlighted to US policymakers the security risks *to* North American economic integration that were in some part inherent *in* North American economic integration. The impacts of 9/11 went far beyond the tragic loss of life. Subsequent border closures and heightened security imposed high costs on North American business, individuals and, more broadly, US interests rooted in regional trilateral economic openness. As the DoHS put it, "the

92. See Christopher Layne, *The Peace of Illusions: American Grand Strategy from 1940 to the Present* (Ithaca, NY: Cornell University Press, 2006), p. 36.

93. *Ibid.*, pp. 34–35, 194–201.

systems that provide the functions essential for a thriving society are increasingly intricate and interconnected. This means that potential disruptions to a system are not fully understood and can have large and unanticipated cascading effects throughout American security."[94] Given the potential terrorist use of "porous" borders[95] and the networks established by *coyotes* and traffickers, it is perhaps inevitable, and somewhat understandable, that terrorism, immigration and drugs have been conflated. There remains little hard evidence of the much vaunted threat of terrorists actually crossing the US–Mexico border. However, considering the political and economic ramifications if the "millennium bomber" Ahmed Ressam had not been stopped by a vigilant customs inspector at the US–Canadian border en route to bomb Los Angeles International Airport should give us pause regarding the threat to continued integration from such potential cross-border incidents. The conundrum for US policymakers is therefore not just how to maintain the advantages of economic integration and openness in the NAFTA zone and to secure the border, but to secure that very economic openness. Placing our discussion above within this context in fact helps us to understand some of the policy incoherence with regard to the apparent failure to meet US strategic goals at the border itself. The border paradox can only be fully understood when we consider economic and security interests as dovetailed rather than distinct. Regional openness is in the US's strategic interest and thus must be secured; securing it at the border hurts regional openness.[96]

Mexico's security crisis also plays into this dilemma. We therefore need to understand what exactly it is about drug-related violence that threatens US interests. The literature we have summarised here has often emphasised the complex domestic drivers of drug policy through the kind of congressional discourse and legislative pressure we saw above, as well as bureaucratic inertia.[97] Of course, in much of the official documentation the public health and security of citizens in both countries is held up as a key CN policy rationale.[98] However, we would be better placed to understand a significant portion of the drug-related violence in Mexico as directly contradictory to US strategic interests in economic integration and the NAFTA space. Although not as intense, widespread or ideological as "traditional" political violence, in areas of states like Michoacán, Tamaulipas, Nuevo León and Guerrero the violence in Mexico is akin to low-level insurgency, with attacks on the state commonplace.[99] In any case, while we may quibble

94. US Department of Homeland Security, *Risk Management Fundamentals*, *op. cit.*, p. 7.

95. Serrano, *op. cit.*, pp. 616–617.

96. Interestingly, a report by the Council on Foreign Relations in 2005 (of which Robert Pastor was a co-author) made this very point and seemed to acknowledge the inherent dilemma involved in securing economic openness. See Council on Foreign Relations, "Building a North American Community", May 2005, pp. 3–4 and 7–11; available: <http://www.cfr.org/canada/building-north-american-community/p8102> (accessed 11 August 2014).However, much of the debate continues to revolve around an unhelpful distinction between "economics" and "security."

97. For example, Gilbert, *op. cit.*, pp. 204–205.

98. US Department of State, *Joint Statement on the Mérida Initiative*, *op. cit.*; US State Department Bureau of Western Hemisphere Affairs, *Managing our 21st Century Border: Fact Sheet*, *op. cit.*

99. For academic/journalistic cases that outline the existence of this phenomenon, see Ioan Grillo, *El Narco: Inside Mexico's Criminal Insurgency* (London: Bloomsbury Press, 2012); Killebrew, *op. cit.*; John P. Sullivan and Robert J. Bunker (eds.), *Mexico's Criminal Insurgency* (Bloomington, IN: Universe Books/Small Wars Foundation, 2012).

over a precise definition, the instability generated by the violence is a genuine strategic concern. Several cables have discussed at least the potential for instability related to drug trafficking violence to impact upon economic investment and wider business and trade inside Mexico itself.[100]

Andreas and Friman have highlighted how increasingly powerful transnational criminal actors, through their increased use of violence, can undermine the authority of the state both by directly challenging it and by undermining the population's wider trust in the state and its institutions.[101] The emergence of vigilante groups in Mexico is a public expression of disaffection with the state's security-providing abilities, and an indicator that this process is already taking place in certain areas (again especially Michoacán and Guerrero). A Mexican state unable to effectively hold the monopoly of violence or guarantee the rule of law is inimical to the interests of the US in sustaining an open economically integrated investment environment in the NAFTA zone. In the context of Mexico's security crisis, US border concerns are not primarily about "spillover violence" or the effects of drugs themselves (although of course these, alongside other considerations, factor into policymaking). Instead, the manner in which the profits that are massively swelled in the act of successfully crossing illicit material over the border act as a force multiplier for the operational abilities of violent groups inside Mexico. These profits connect US interests at the border to these wider interests in Mexico itself. This concern co-exists with the US interest in preventing potential terror threats from emanating from Mexico and crossing the border. Of course, the paradox that integration and border security appear to be aiding drug trafficking groups in this force multiplication resurfaces once again here.

Making the case for compounded strategic interests both at the heart of US policy and at the heart of the paradox identified above is not to dismiss the other arguments I have utilised here. This is not least because I agree that domestic politics and the complexity of the US state have played a large role in the seemingly ever-increasing focus on border security. Much of my argument here could perhaps be more applicable to what we may call the executive level of the US state than the complex, legislation-producing congressional level, which contains a large border security "caucus," as we saw above. The issue of immigration especially muddies the waters, as migration itself has been defined as a threat apart from terrorism, and this has created further security interests in myriad ways across political scales.[102] While we certainly do not want to define interests as pre-given and simply rationally accessible, however, neither do we want to reduce them to ideational or discursive constructs. I hope I have shown in this section that there are strategic interests at play here. Thus, the contradictions that have arisen from attempts to ensure the US strategic interest in an economically secure border that both promotes economic

100. For evidence of both US concern in this area and descriptions about how former President Calderón explained his own security crackdown in these terms, see US Embassy Mexico, *Scene Setter for President's Trip to Mexico, March 12–14th, 2007*, Cable Reference: 001102 (5 March 2007), available: <http://www.cablegatesearch.net/cable.php?id=07MEXICO1102&q=merida%20mexico> (accessed 3 October 2012); US Embassy Mexico, *Effect of Violence on Mexican Investment*, Cable Reference: 001536 (22 March 2006), available: <http://www.cablegatesearch.net/cable.php?id=06MEXICO1536&q=investment%20mexico%20security> (accessed 4 October 2012).

101. Friman and Andreas, "Introduction", *op. cit.*, p. 13.

102. Jason Ackleson, "Constructing Security on the US–Mexico Border", *Political Geography*, Vol. 24, No. 2 (2005), pp. 165–184.

integration and protects it from potential threats are more an indication of the quixotic nature of achieving this at the south-west border itself than the fallout between competing or contradictory distinct policy goals championed by easily definable groups. This has led the US, especially at an executive level, to seek policy alternatives in projecting border security into Mexico, both to relieve security pressure at the border and to protect strategic interests in North American security.

The Mérida Initiative and Transnational Organised Crime: Towards North American Security?

Many of the analysts we have highlighted here have discussed the potential for and nascent moves towards a wider conception of North American security that integrates security policy across the three NAFTA countries to catch up with economic integration, and indeed some have actively encouraged such a development. Others have discussed concepts such as "border projection," whereby the US achieves border security through aiding its international partners. However, they have also, for the most part, remained sceptical that these processes are either currently happening in North America or indeed will happen in the near future. Pastor charges that "[t]oday's problems" in the NAFTA area, including continuing security problems, "are the result of the three governments' failure to govern the North American space."[103] He encourages the creation of trilateral institutions to tackle security issues, including CN concerns. O'Neil suggests a partnership-based approach to mutual security issues that would move beyond the militaristic focus of the Mérida Initiative to something akin to a "whole of society" programme that seeks to tackle Mexico's security crisis from the perspective of inculcating Mexican "rule of law."[104] Andreas has discussed the potential for the creation of a North American security perimeter in line with policy initiatives that have suggested "pushing borders outwards" as a solution to the border paradox, whereby border security tasks could be completed by trusted international partners, in this case Canada and Mexico.[105] However he has concluded that such an approach "would require such a high level of institutionalization and regional policy harmonization that it does not seem realistic at the present time" and instead through piecemeal policy programmes the potential creation "of an informal, quasi-continental security perimeter" could eventually take place.[106]

These arguments are important and well made. Nonetheless, they have missed (in fairness in some cases due to their time of writing) that much of the policy undertaken through and "around" the Mérida Initiative is designed to ensure that the Mexican state is far more competent in meeting a wide variety of current and potential security threats. This is very much inclusive of, but not limited to, CN concerns and the strategic threat of Mexican instability. This aids in the attempted establishment of a North American security perimeter, to help a US one beleaguered by the problems we have identified. Official explanations of

103. Pastor, *op. cit.*, p. 167.

104. O'Neil, *Two Nations*, *op. cit.*, pp. 159–164.

105. Andreas, "Redrawing the Line", *op. cit.*, pp. 98–99.

106. *Ibid.*

policy have emphasised that the US is partnering with Mexico as part of a wider concern in ensuring that it can "leverage opportunities working with our foreign partners to intercept and neutralize threats before they reach the US border."[107] The policy reaction to Mexico's current security crisis is very much a part of this, and indeed drug-related violence has acted as a catalyst for policy action. However, it has also acted as a vehicle for a longer-term goal to improve North American security through "border projection" and a NAFTA perimeter. In notable ways, Mérida provided an avenue for the "security" element of the defunct trilateral Security and Prosperity Partnership (SPP).[108] The SPP was described by former Assistant Secretary for Western Hemisphere Affairs Thomas Shannon as an agreement about understanding "North America as a shared economic space and that as a shared economic space we need to protect it." The SPP would effectively "armor NAFTA."[109] As the SPP slowly unravelled under popular pressure and policy inertia, Mérida became a politically expedient conduit for US efforts to create greater security in Mexico even as more trilateral options stalled.

The rhetorical language surrounding US policy in Mexico, or perhaps more accurately official discourse, has reflected the above. The Mérida Initiative has also coalesced with the emergence of TOC as a significant focus within US strategy. Much of the academic analysis of TOC has been critical of it as a concept.[110] I would certainly agree that it is problematically defined within both academic and official parameters. However, the point I want to emphasise here is that the increasing emphasis on TOC in the Mexican context, running through policy academia, military statements and administrative policy programmes like the *Strategy to Combat Transnational Organized Crime*,[111] is reflective of the security challenge facing the US. Where US strategic interests in Mexico are facilitated by the open North American economic space, while drug trafficking groups straddle and take advantage of those open borders, focusing on transnational threats makes *prima facie* sense. Effectively, the very "transnationalism" of this challenge necessitates a response that goes beyond the immediate border with Mexico. The use of TOC here then is part of the wider concrete move to solutions that transcend border security by looking at the security issues more regionally and holistically. As a Pacific Council report noted, drug trafficking is not "a 'border problem', but rather a bi-national and international problem that governments try to address *in part* through enforcement and interdiction at the border."[112]

---

107. Testimony of Mariko Silver, then Acting Assistant Secretary, Office of International Affairs, DoHS, *Merida Part Two: Insurgency and Terrorism in Mexico, op. cit.*, p. 30.

108. M. Angeles Villarreal and Jennifer E. Lake, *Security and Prosperity Partnership of North America: An Overview and Selected Issues* (Congressional Research Service, May 2009), p. 1.

109. Shannon quoted in Laura Carlsen, "Armoring NAFTA: The Battleground for Mexico's Future", NACLA Report on the Americas 41,5 (September–October 2008), p. 17.

110. For example, Michael Woodiwiss, "Transnational Organised Crime: The Global Reach of an American Concept", in Adam Edwards and Pete Gill (eds.), *Transnational Organised Crime: Perspectives on Global Security* (London: Routledge, 2006), pp. 14–20.

111. US White House: National Security Council, *The Strategy to Combat Transnational Organized Crime* (Washington, DC, 2010); US Department of Defense, *Counternarcotics & Global Threats Strategy* (Washington, DC, 2011).

112. Pacific Council on International Policy, *Managing the United States–Mexico Border: Cooperative Solutions to Common Challenges* (Los Angeles, CA, 13 November 2009), p. 10; emphasis added.

We can see the depth of the effort to go beyond the US–Mexico border briefly in some concrete policy detail.[113] For example, and perhaps most obviously, we can highlight how Mérida policies are directly aimed to help Mexico to achieve greater border security at its southern borders as part of a policy to extend security perimeters and relieve security pressures at the US–Mexico border. Thus, the Mérida Initiative builds on previous US programmes by financially assisting Mexican institutions such as the National Migration Institute (INM, previously INAMI) and Secretariat of Communications (SCT) to help improve their security, IT, inspection, verification and database systems. Mérida monies were also to be directed to Mexico's intelligence service, Centro de Investigación y Seguridad Nacional (CISEN) for "enhanced data management and analysis capabilities."[114] Mérida policy detail confirms that these programmes went ahead, and we can see the focus on regional border security in that detail. Another report of the Senate Foreign Relations Committee confirmed that Mérida funds were pending for biometric equipment and biometric sites for INM, including for 10 locations along the southern border.[115] This equipment was used to log persons crossing the border and has been touted for its part in allowing INM to track these individuals more efficiently, and potentially to "identify individuals in immigration detention centers who might pose a threat to national security."[116]

Mérida also intersects with wider programmes and border security interests that go beyond what we may commonly think of as "border security." The US's Export Control and Related Border Security (EXBS) Program (which grew out of nuclear non-proliferation efforts in former Soviet satellites, and has since expanded to a role in helping states to meet the non-proliferation obligations of UN Resolution 1540[117] and building general export controls for conventional weaponry)[118] has intersected with Mérida, with the Initiative helping the US to "set the conditions for development in the nonproliferation arena in Mexico."[119] Underlining how Mérida is an integral part of joined up security policy in Mexico and North America, "the US Department of Energy's (DOE) Megaports and Second Line of Defense (SLD) nuclear non-proliferation programs have worked in concert with Merida [and] also complemented the EXBS program and facilitated its success."[120] This is a specific example of US efforts to improve trade controls for all kinds of illicit smuggling, where Mexico is a key site for action. Crucially, the

113. It should be noted that this is a contextually selected overview from a wider research project, and there is in fact a far wider empirical case for the conclusions I have drawn here.

114. US Department of State, *FY2008 Supplemental Appropriation Spending Plan: Mexico, Central America Haiti and the Dominican Republic* (Washington, DC, 2008), p. 6.

115. *Common Enemy, Common Struggle, op. cit.*, p. 20.

116. US Embassy Mexico, "US Delivers New Biometric Technology to INM to Help Strengthen Mexico's Southern Border", Press Release, 3 November 2011, available: <http://mexico.usembassy.gov/press-releases/ep111004-inami.html> (accessed 3 October 2012).

117. For further information see the website of the UN Security Council's 1540 Committee, at <http://www.un.org/en/sc/1540/>.

118. US Department of State, *The EXBS Program*, available: <http://www.state.gov/t/isn/ecc/c27911.htm> (accessed 29 May 2013).

119. US Department of State, *EXBS Newsletter*, Vol. II, No. 3 (Washington, DC, July 2011), available: <http://www.state.gov/documents/organization/170969.pdf> (accessed 29 May 2013).

120. *Ibid.* Also see US Department of Energy, National Nuclear Security Administration, *Fact Sheet: NNSA's Second Line of Defense Program* (Washington, DC, February 2011) and US Department of Energy, National Nuclear Security Administration, *Megaports Initiative, 2010* (Washington, DC, September 2010).

US is at least attempting to enhance its Mexican partner's capacity to improve trade controls within its own territory. Thus, it not seeks a potentially safer environment for the (admittedly small) amount of trade that comes into Mexico before entering the US,[121] as well as generalised improved capacity in Mexico, but also aims to help defend Mexico from possible illicit threats emanating from trade as part of the North American economic zone. This itself is indicative of a wider strategy to ensure that "efforts to secure our borders [...] also include efforts to secure global trade and travel networks" in a manner that ensures "both economic competitiveness and national security."[122]

This is a good point at which to note that non-Mérida security funding for Mexico has also increased in tandem with the Initiative itself. However, the nature of the Initiative and this non-Initiative funding clearly demonstrate that the US is concerned with both its strategic interests inside Mexico and in helping to solve the border paradox through pushing security outwards. Thus, Department of Defense (DoD) programmes aid Mexican security inside its territory, and intersect with the wider goals of Mérida. Under DoD aid programmes such as Section 1004 Counter Drug Assistance and Section 1206 Train and Equip Authority,[123] the Pentagon increased its involvement in aid provision to Mexico. For example in FY 2008, the DoD provided just under $12.5 million to the Mexican government in a "CT package" designed to provide "[e]quipment and training to reduce ungoverned territories that could be exploited by terrorists as safe havens and transit points."[124] Much of this DoD aid has been administered through US Northern Command (USNORTHCOM), the Operational Command created in the wake of 9/11, charged with "homeland security" and securing US interests in Mexico and portions of the Caribbean. Former Commander General Victor Renuart did not draw a particularly sharp distinction between his comments on Mexico's CN concerns related to "organized violent criminal networks" and the rationale for the 1206 "CT" package, explaining that its equipment provision "includes personal protective equipment, digital media forensics equipment, night vision devices, and equipment needed to board suspect vessels at sea."[125] Thus, the militarised threat of drug traffickers, among potential others, is significantly met with a militarised response. However, it has also been under 1004 authority that Mexican personnel have been trained in container inspection and port security, again reflecting a "border projection" philosophy.[126]

121. As Pastor makes an issue of throughout *The North American Idea, op. cit.*, this kind of trading is limited by the lack of a common external tariff, imposing extra costs upon it.

122. Testimony of Mariko Silver, then Acting Assistant Secretary, Office of International Affairs, DoHS, *Merida Part Two: Insurgency and Terrorism in Mexico, op. cit.*, p. 30.

123. These are relatively long-running DoD aid programmes authorised by Congress. They operate with a good deal of autonomy from congressional oversight. The former is ostensibly a CN programme, the latter a CT one.

124. US Department of Defense, *Section 1209 and Section 1203(b) Report to Congress on Foreign Assistance Related Programs for Fiscal Years, 2008, 2009 and 2010* (Washington, DC, 2012), p. 100.

125. "Statement of General Victor E. Renuart Jr., USAF Commander United States Northern Command and North American Aerospace Defense Command" before the Senate Armed Services Committee, 111th Congress (17 March 2009).

126. US Department of State and US Department of Defense, *Foreign Military Training Fiscal Years 2008–2009: Volume I* (Washington, DC, 2010), p. 156; and *Foreign Military Training Fiscal Years 2009–2010: Volume I* (Washington, DC, 2011), p. 154.

Conclusion: The Border Paradox (Reprise?)

We have seen that the border has in many senses become a paradoxical space in that the US seeks to utilise it as both a site of enhanced economic interchange and a security barrier thwarting a number of threats. These threats transmuted into a broader focus on border security. We saw that analysts have both highlighted the problems this has caused and sought to explain this apparent paradox. For many this is evidence that the border is increasingly becoming a site of a domestic political clash between divergent economic and security prerogatives. I have sought to explain how there is significant convergence on the need to create an economically secure border, based on the association between economic and security interests, into what we may term strategic interests. However, this is an inherently difficult undertaking. I have then briefly shown how US policy has moved further towards security integration based on creating a security perimeter that recognises the connectivity in North America, and the strategic importance of the NAFTA zone to US interests. Thus, this development is both a reflection of a strategic imperative and a possible way to solve the border paradox through the extension of borders and the meeting of threats inside Mexico.

However, we should conclude on a note of caution. Contingencies may very well define the future of the US–Mexico partnership and the wider project of North American economic integration. Additionally, there are some factors that will likely stall the move to security integration. The border remains a crucial space within NAFTA where asymmetries and inequalities of power and wealth meet, and integration will continue to fuel security problems that will be deemed to require a response. The difficulty in creating an economically secure border will likely mean inadvertent missteps, especially when combined with the vagaries of domestic politics, political interests and bureaucratic politics. Mérida itself contained "traditional" border security programmes. Thus, the border paradox itself remains a key challenge. In addition, there is now a powerful lobby for continuing escalation of homeland security at the border, and distinctive interests within that lobby. Given the economic boon to private companies and certain institutions and regions through increased border security and attendant equipment, there is a case for seeing a certain kind of "homeland security Keynesianism" active on the border. What impact this will have on economic interests and trade remains to be seen. Finally, the relationship between the US and Mexico itself is key. For example, should Mexico seek to assert its independence from US drug policy, or corruption and/or lack of progress "on the ground" begin to frustrate the US to an intolerable degree, it is possible that the continuing progress towards security integration will become stalled, and the border paradox loom large once more.

Acknowledgements

Many thanks to Professor Larry Herzog and Professor Keith Hayward for affording me the opportunity to contribute to this special issue, and for their input and comments throughout the process. Thanks also to Dr. Ruth Blakeley for her comments on earlier drafts, and Dr. Doug Stokes and Dr. Jonathan Joseph for their guidance on wider research that has informed the work here. Also thanks to Molly Molloy for her help and work on casualties in Mexico's drug violence. Finally, thanks to Elizabeth Ashby for proofreading and Dr. Govinda Clayton for advice on style. All final work, and thereby any error within it, is entirely mine.

Index

For Product Safety Concerns and Information please contact our EU representative GPSR@taylorandfrancis.com Taylor & Francis Verlag GmbH, Kaufingerstraße 24, 80331 München, Germany

Batch number: 08153807

Printed by Printforce, the Netherlands